Facing Death

Embracing Life

UNDERSTANDING *What Dying People Want*

David Kuhl, M.D.

DOUBLEDAY CANADA

Parts of Chapter Nine, "Experiencing Spirituality at the End of Life," will appear in *Journal of Cancer Education*, Vol. 21, Number 1a.

Doubleday Canada and colophon are trademarks.

LIBRARY AND ARCHIVES CANADA CATALOGUING IN PUBLICATION

Kuhl, David
    Facing death, embracing life : understanding what
dying people want / David Kuhl.

Includes bibliographical references.

ISBN-13: 978-0-385-66066-2
ISBN-10:0-385-66066-9

    1. Death–Psychological aspects. 2. Terminally ill–Psychology.
3. Terminally ill–Family relationships. I. Title.

BF789.D4K83 2006   155.9'37   C2005-907130-3

Text design: CS Richardson
Printed and bound in Canada

Published in Canada by
Doubleday Canada, a division of
Random House of Canada Limited

Visit Random House of Canada Limited's website: www.randomhouse.ca

TRANS   10   9   8   7   6   5   4   3   2   1

To the people who participated in my research project
and thereby became my teachers

To Jean, Jennifer and Sarah

Contents

Introduction

I ended my first book, *What Dying People Want*, with a description of my perspective on the final days of my sister's life. As I write these words, several years have passed since Nancy died. Surrounded by family members, I trust that she knew how much we loved her, because we all had a chance to tell her. I remember my time with her as if it happened yesterday.

Through the last weeks of Nancy's life I was challenged to face mortality in my own family—was the work I had been doing merely a research project or were the lessons I had learned pertinent to the situation? I knew at that moment that the people I had known in my work over the previous fifteen years and those who had participated in the research project had given me an incredible gift in offering their stories to me. Those stories provided guidance through some very difficult days. The gift of their stories made a significant difference to Nancy's journey, as well as to the journey of my whole family. We were able to do and say what needed to be done and said. For that, I will be forever grateful. Another gift that was given to me through the work I did with people at the end of life was the realization that what dying people want is the same as what living people want, primarily a sense of connection to themselves, to those they love and who love them, and to a sense or essence of something greater than themselves. Physical pain, poor communication and anxiety are some of the features that impede the process of connection. For many people, knowing that they have a terminal illness serves as a catalyst for them to search for meaning, to make sense of their lives, to appreciate and be honest with themselves and with those they love.

I wrote the last chapters of the book shortly after Nancy's death. During that time, I experienced a lot of emotions, one of which was anger. "I was angry and frustrated with a system that seemed to allow her to slip through the cracks. In fact, at one point I was filled with rage. I understand the system, and I understand that things happen unintentionally. These same things have happened to people under my care over the years. But I understand it differently now. The system will never be perfect, but because it was my sister, I wanted perfection for her." People at the end of life can benefit from the company of others who share that time with them, people who work hard to know and understand the needs and desires of the person at the end of life in the context of a complex health-care system, people who are willing and prepared to act as advocates on behalf of the person with the terminal illness.

I was also angry at myself for waiting. "One would think that fifteen years of being with people who are dying, listening to the stories of their lives through a research project, and writing a book about it would be enough to teach me that waiting is a risky business," I wrote then. I remember how Nancy and

I decided to meet at a palliative care conference in Prince Albert, Saskatchewan, several years before Nancy died. She was a palliative care nurse, so she had good reason to be there. In part she attended so we could meet. It was a meeting of adult siblings. It was the first conversation we had in the absence of our spouses and children. We had our first interaction about who we were and who we had become as adults since we left home. After she died, I was very sad that the opportunity for more conversations like that never happened. We certainly had more conversations, but never again were they quite as intimate as that time in Prince Albert. I was angry and deeply disappointed that distance, time and apprehension had prevented us from cultivating our adult relationship. That was part of my grief.

I remember writing about my experience of feeling anger toward Nancy. (I still feel an awkwardness about saying that.) "I'm angry at her for her being so private, so independent, so alone in her suffering that she didn't invite me to stop waiting and come to be with her. But I know that I need to respect her for being the private person she was. I know that anger is part of grief, but it feels that we ought not to be angry at those who have died. I'm angry because I love her and I miss her. I am working to forgive myself for waiting too long. I know she knew I loved her and I know that she loved me—that's the beginning of forgiveness." I certainly respect the choices she made, as they were her choices. I am no longer angry at her. My understanding and appreciation of who she was in my life has only grown over time. And, I still miss her. I believe I will continue to miss her for as long as I live. That emotion is testimony to who she was in my life and now serves as a reminder of the value of our relationship.

If I had to do it again, would I do anything differently? Absolutely. In one sense the course of Nancy's illness was like a chronic disease. It went on for nine years, and I believed it could continue for considerably longer than it did. I waited too long to deepen my relationship with her. It's my hope that this book will prevent you from doing the same thing I did, that is, waiting too long to have meaningful conversations and discussions with people who are important to you, especially if you or they have a terminal illness, a chronic illness, or may simply be getting on in years. This book follows on from my first book. So if you have read my first book, this companion will likely seem very familiar to you. You may wish to refer to that book from time to time, but it won't be necessary, as the stories and content I have used here will be sufficient to understand their context. The chapters of this companion work are matched to the chapters in the book. I hope it will feel like the company of an old friend. It is also my hope that it will serve to equip and guide you in a practical way through the process of living with a terminal illness, either your own or that of someone you love. It may also serve to guide you through a process of reflecting on features of your life that would be important to you if you had a terminal illness. There is space for you to record your history, your thoughts, your wishes. This book could be used as a journal, as a record, a workbook, a companion to the original book, and/or as a guide to usher you through this time in your life. I have extracted some of the stories, information and exercises from the first book and put them into a manual format to enhance the practicality of this book.

I believe that people who know they are dying have something very important, very truthful, to say. In listening to the stories of people who have been told they had six to twelve months of life to live, I learned that a process of life review emerges, that they long to belong, that they want to speak their truth and often don't know how or where to begin, that they want to know who they are and who they were, and that they experience the transcendent in ways that give them a sense of meaning, purpose and value. I wish I had really understood all those things three years before Nancy died, at the time when there was a change in her disease process. I also wish I had said that if ever she wanted to explore or talk about any of those things, I would be honored to listen and to work hard to understand who she was as an adult who happened to be my sister.

I write about this again because I believe it is a common experience. People continue to say these same things about living with a terminal illness. Perhaps it is especially common among those who live with a chronic illness or a terminal illness of a lengthy duration. My sense is that it is also common for people who are simply growing older. But if the knowledge of a terminal illness serves as an impetus to begin to look back over one's life, when do the people without that message begin the process? And when do those who care for them and about them begin to address issues that might concern either party? (That is a challenge for many people today and will become more common with the changing demographics in this country.) The only answer I can come up with is that it is never too early to connect with the people we care about. I am also aware that it might be very difficult and in some instances awkward to do so. It requires a willingness on the part of both parties, that is, both people in a relationship are responsible to that relationship for being honest and open, for speaking truthfully, and for exchanging information, feelings and concerns. It also requires courage, focus, creating an opportunity, and time to spend in the relationship. If you've got something you would like to say to someone before you or that person dies, it is likely important enough to say right now. And for some people you know, it might be important or of value to say something to them regardless of whether either one of you has a diagnosis of a terminal illness.

ONE

Time and Anxiety

Time

Brent, one of my greatest teachers about living with a terminal illness, told me that "talking about death is very difficult for a lot of us in the beginning." Death is a reality for all of us. And yet for many it is a reality that lies dormant within us. Some of you know that reality because you have been told that you have a terminal illness. Some of you have been told you have a terminal illness, yet still do not know that reality. And some of you know that reality for reasons other than having a terminal illness—perhaps because someone in your life has died.

Life is full of dying; life is full of death. When the reality of death strikes, it may strike with a "roar of awakening," an awakening that reminds us of our physical limitations, of the value of our relationships, and of the depth of our spirit. We may regret that much time has passed and yet be thankful that we have a new beginning, an awareness that while we are in the shadow of death, a new life has begun.

It is certain that all of us will die. We hope and plan for

a long and healthy life, and may even be fortunate enough to fulfill those hopes, but life will come to an end eventually. There are no exemptions, no exceptions—life is terminal. And at the same time, people who are dying are still living. In a sense, there is value in appreciating that people who are living are dying, and people who are dying are living—an obvious concept and yet one we are shy to entertain or embrace. If we fear dying, do we also fear living? If we fear death, do we fear life? Perhaps we cannot live authentically until we confront our own mortality. Marjorie, an elderly woman with cancer, stated that "despite having a terminal illness, one is alive. After confronting death, every day is a miracle."

Before you begin this exercise, you might want to make yourself physically comfortable in a space that will allow you to be private and uninterrupted. You may choose to record your responses, using this book as a journal.

Your first memory of death likely colors subsequent experiences that pertain to dying and death. What is your first memory of death? Was it someone you knew well, a family member or a friend, an acquaintance, a member of your church or your community who died? Perhaps it was a pet? It might have been a news item you heard on the radio, or perhaps the death of a celebrity you saw on television.

Was it tragic? Was it an accidental death, a homicide or a suicide?

_____

_____

_____

What was that experience like for you? What did you feel? Have those feelings changed? If so, how?

_____

_____

_____

_____

_____

Who was present when you first learned about it?

_____

_____

Did you have an opportunity to say goodbye to the person? What did you say? What was left unsaid? What do you wish you had said? If you had one more opportunity to speak to that person, what would you say?

_____

_____

_____

_____

_____

_____

What effect did the death have on you at the time, and what effect did it have on the people you were living with at the time?

How did that death affect your life? Your impression of the end of life? Your experience of ritual? Who or what helped you to understand the event? Who or what gave you comfort at that time?

What did you learn from the experience that might be of value to you today?

For most people, the experience and perception of time changes once they have been informed of having a terminal illness. At one level we may all know that we are dying. At another level we don't dare to entertain thoughts of death and dying, as it seems that we might be courting the process. Only people with a terminal illness know what it means to live with that illness. Those of us who care for them are left to work hard to understand the experience. How might we begin to do so? Using our best communication skills, listening, checking with them about our understanding, being with them in silence, participating, and observing their experiences are all ways to come to understand the life of a person with a terminal illness.

Before we consider what it might be like to learn about having a terminal illness, think about features of the past that have contributed to who you are today. This exercise can be done on your own, with a friend, or in a group. Consider a timeline. This might also be called a "life-line." On a sheet of unlined paper, draw a six-inch line: it can be horizontal, diagonal or vertical. It can also be a circle, if you prefer that. On the left side of the line, or the "beginning" of the circle, write the word Birth, on the right side of the line or at the end of the circle, write the word Death.

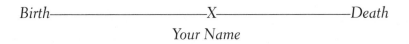

Birth———————————X———————————*Death*
Your Name

Think of this line as representing your lifetime. Consider your family history, including the longevity of your parents and/or grandparents. Include your own history of illness/well-being. Place an X on the line to indicate where you believe you are at present. That is, if you believe that you have lived half of your life, place the X midway between Birth and Death. If you believe that you have lived two-thirds of your life, place the X two-thirds of the way along the line. Once you have placed the X on the line, write your name below the X. Then take note of your feelings.

- Is it difficult to write your name below the X? Do you wonder whether it ought to be placed at a different spot? Do you have a sense of relief? Of anxiety? Of fear? Or a realization that much of your life has passed?

_____

_____

_____

_____

_____

Next think of six significant events, relationships, or inner processes in your life: examples would be meeting your spouse or partner, the birth of a child, the death of a friend, an exciting vacation, a failure, a good financial investment, graduation from university, the birth of a grandchild, a car accident. Number the events 1 through 6 and list them below. Then place the numbers on the line between your birth and the X.

1. _____
2. _____
3. _____
4. _____
5. _____
6. _____

- What emotions do you feel about each of those events?
- What about the emotion you feel about your life as a whole?
- Are you satisfied with the life you have lived so far?
- Do you wish that some things had been different?
- Are there events that ought to have been placed on the line but, because of the pain they caused you, you omitted them?
- What emotions do you feel as you spend time reflecting on these questions? (When asked these questions people often say they feel emotional. If possible, name the emotion, e.g., sad, content, happy, encouraged.)

Focus on the line between the X and Death.

- How might you best embrace life in the time that remains?
- If you didn't have to live up to the expectations of anyone else, how would you live, and who would you be?
- Are there things you would like to do? Places you would like to visit? People you would like to spend more time with? Conversations you would like to have? Events you would like to attend—the baptism of a grandchild, the graduation of your eldest child, a birthday, a bar mitzvah, a wedding, an anniversary?

_____

_____

_____

_____

_____

_____

_____

_____

Choose six events, relationships or inner processes that you anticipate experiencing in the future and list them below. Number the events, beginning with the number 7, and place those numbers on the line between the X and Death.

7. _____

8. _____

9. _____

10. _____

11. _____

12 _____

- How do you feel about each of those events, the people involved in them, and your life as a whole?
- What are the emotions you experience as you spend time thinking about the future?

_____

_____

_____

_____

_____

_____

This exercise has taken you through the past years of your life and into the future. It is a relatively benign exercise. For the most part, it is designed to remind you of memories that you treasure. Now, instead of looking back at your whole life, review the events of today. How is it that you are reading this manual? What led you to purchase it or to pick it up to read it today? What were you doing before you picked it up? How would your life be different if you were told today that you had a terminal illness? Only you know the answer to that question and it may be difficult to find the answer.

We order our lives by chronological time. It is exactly the same for each of us, sixty seconds in a minute, sixty minutes in an hour, twenty-four hours in a day, seven days in a week . . . until one day we learn that we have a terminal illness. At that moment, time seems to stop. We don't hear the ticking anymore. The time that remains takes on new meaning. We may experience our past, present and future in a different way. And we may begin to realize that the only time we have is now.

Imagine the scenario in which your family physician informs you today that the symptoms you have experienced and he has been investigating are those of a terminal illness. Unfortunately, there are no known treatments that can reverse the disease process. Some of the medications available may slow the disease, but none of them are known to arrest it. You are told that your life expectancy is six to twelve months. From the moment you hear those words, time changes.

- How do you feel? Try to be as specific as you can be with regard to the emotion you feel.

....

....

....

....

In essence, the information given to you by the physician has moved the X from where you believed it to be to a place much closer to Death. In order to begin to understand that experience, I invite you to draw another timeline. This time, place the X one centimeter from the righthand end of the line:

Birth————————————————————————*X—Death*

Your Name

Write your name below the X. What are your emotions as you place the X closer to Death than you did on the previous exercise? Does it seem real to you?

....

....

....

Again think of six significant events, relationships, or inner processes in your life, and list them below. Number the events 1 through 6 and place the numbers on the line between Birth and the X.

1. ....

2. ....

3. ....

4. ....

5. ....

6. ....

Consider the same questions as before:
- What emotions do you feel about each of those events?
- How did each of those events, relationships or inner processes contribute to who you are today?
- How do you feel about your life as a whole?
- Are you satisfied with the life you have lived?
- Do you wish that some things had been different?
- Are there events that ought to have been placed on the line but, because of the pain they caused you, you omitted them?
- What are the emotions you feel as you spend time reflecting on these questions?

....

....

....

....

....

....

Focus on the line between the X and Death.

- How might you best embrace life in the time that remains?
- If you didn't have to live up to the expectations of anyone else, how would you live, who would you be?
- Are there things you would like to do? Places you would like to visit? People you would like to spend more time

with? Conversations you would like to have? Events you would like to attend—the baptism of a grandchild, the graduation of your eldest child, a birthday, a bar mitzvah, a wedding, an anniversary?

....
....
....
....
....
....

Choose six events, relationships or inner processes that you anticipate experiencing in the future. Number the events beginning with the number 7 and place those numbers on the line between the X and Death.

7. ....
8. ....
9. ....
10 ....
11. ....
12. ....

- How do you feel about each of those events, the people involved in them, and your life as a whole?
- What are you feeling as you spend time thinking about the future?
- If you knew that the prediction of having six months to a year to live was accurate, would you live differently? Starting when?

- Would you care as much about what other people think about you, or about what you do, and how you live?
- How would you fill your time?
- How does the new reality affect the answers to your questions in the previous timeline exercise?
- What effect does this have on your feelings?
- What about unfinished activities? Are they still important to you?
- Are there other activities that seem important, now that you have only six to twelve months remaining in this world?

- And what about looking back over your life? Does the knowledge that you are living with a terminal illness change your feelings about your memories?
- Are there other relationships or events that come to mind as being significant?
- Are there things you wish you had done? Things you wish you had not done?
- Are there conversations that you wish had not happened or had been different?
- Do you wish you had said some things that you did not say?

....

....

....

....

....

....

....

....

....

If you truly know that you have a limited amount of time remaining, you may become aware of events that you will miss. With that realization, there will likely be a sense of loss and grief. You may want to write a letter or dictate a message to someone to be opened or listened to in the future. For example, if you think that you might miss a birthday, a wedding, a graduation, or any other celebration, you could write a letter to the individual who is significant to you in that event. If you are a parent who will miss your child's graduation from high school or university, you might write a letter to be opened on graduation day. If you are a grandparent who will miss the birth of a grandchild, you could write a whole series of letters that could be opened periodically by your grandchild. The letters could include information about yourself, your childhood, and features of the family history that you feel are important for the next generation of family members to know. In carrying out such activities, your grief and despair may turn to mourning and hope.

Time never stops. However, life ends, and in that sense,

time stops. And yet we live our lives as though we will endure forever. People are growing old and dying all around us, yet we think it will not happen to us. Death happens only to others, those who are older, those of our parents' generations, those who are sick, our neighbors—but not to us. Even people working in health-care facilities live as though death belongs only to others. We believe we have time to spend, time to spare, time to procrastinate, time to waste.

The only time we have is now. That was one of the major lessons I learned in spending time with people who knew they were dying. The moment someone is told that her illness will likely result in death, time changes. Some may hear the message when they are feeling well, unaware of the disease process advancing within their bodies. Others may actually welcome the information in some strange way, because it gives legitimacy to their experience of the previous days, weeks, and months. It helps to make sense of the fatigue, the pain, and the other symptoms that initially infringe on them, then intrude on them, and eventually seem to invade their lives.

It is difficult to imagine what time would be like if we truly had only six to twelve months of life left. Marjorie surprised me with her story, and yet I had heard the same message from many of the people who were patients on the palliative care unit.

Marjorie had lived with cancer for ten years. During the latter stage of her illness, she joined a cancer support group. She spoke of her experience:

> When I'm in the support group and somebody new comes in and says, "I know this is going to sound crazy," I know what they're going to say, and that is: "I'm glad I

FACING DEATH, EMBRACING LIFE

have cancer." I've heard this at least thirty-five times over the years. The reason we say this is because it has turned our lives around, it has made us see what is worthwhile in life and what is a crock, what is not worth worrying about or being angry about. The first time somebody said this, I felt as though she had poured holy water on me. One is left to wonder how anyone could be glad they got a terminal illness. And yet there is a tremendous lesson embedded in the words "it has turned our lives around."

As much as the diagnosis of a terminal illness marks the end of life as it has been known to that point in time, it also serves as a beginning—an opportunity to ask what the time remaining in your life means to you.

- How important is the present—how important is now?
- What does physical, psychological and spiritual well-being mean to me?
- Who is important in my life?
- What is unfinished business for me?
- In what ways would I like to turn my life around?
- What am I able to do and say in the time and with the energy that remain in my lifetime?

....

....

....

....

....

....

There are two concepts of time—measured time (i.e., chrono-logical time) and soulful time–and each is vastly different from the other. Ken Wilber, a psychologist and author, defines soulful time as narrative time, "the time that marks the history of one's own life story or self; the time that carries and re-creates hopes and ideals, plans and ambitions, goals and visions; the subtle time that can speed up or slow down, expand or collapse, transcend or concentrate, according to its interest." This time is marked, in a sense, by the experience of forgetting about measured time. It happens when you are with someone you love and don't realize that hours have passed. It means you are involved in some activity that reflects your true self— a hobby, an interest, and, for some people, their job. It means you are not living up to the expectations of anyone else but rather are simply being you, possessing a renewed awareness of your environment.

Working through this book has to do with reviewing your life story, considering and recreating hopes and ideals, fulfilling plans and ambitions, establishing goals and visions. Perhaps it will serve as a process to concentrate your mind in a new way, to discover features of your life that you may have taken for granted, to confirm your experience of spirituality.

Anxiety

When you are waiting for the doctor's appointment, test results, the diagnosis, the prognosis, or for the treatment to take effect, you are in uncertain circumstances. And with uncertainty you may experience anxiety; the two coexist. Anxiety is a normal and natural response. James Hollis, a Jungian psychologist, defines anxiety as "a free-floating dis-ease that may be activated by nearly anything, may even light for a while on something specific, but that usually originates from the general insecurity one feels in one's life. The level of that insecurity, the amount of anxiety that may be tapped, is partly a function of one's particular history. The more troubled one's environment, family of origin and cultural setting, the more free-floating anxiety will be generated." If you have been with other family members or close friends who had a serious or terminal illness that was anxiety-producing, you may experience a similar anxiety in your present circumstance.

Are you generally an anxious person? What triggers your anxiety? How do you generally experience anxiety? How do you deal with it? How does the anxiety you experience about the disease process going on within you differ from other anxieties you might have had? Has anxiety ever interfered with your ability to live life to its fullest? What would you need to have happen in order to diminish or eliminate your present anxiety?

Hollis differentiates anxiety from fear; he describes fear as being specific, such as the fear of dogs because of being bitten by one as a child, the fear of water because of a near-drowning experience, the fear of heights because of an awareness of the dangers of falling.

It is not surprising that anxiety is part of waiting. You may feel that waiting fills your life with a degree of uncertainty—and so fills your life with anxiety. For some people, waiting fosters impatience and breeds anxiety. Anxiety flourishes amid uncertainty. If you are not familiar with this anxiety because you do not have a terminal illness, think back to your childhood, perhaps when you were learning to swim. At that point, you were most comfortable in the water when you were able to touch the bottom without being in over your head.

The deep end of the pool is a scary place if you are unable to swim to the side of the pool. Likewise, the deeper part of a lake is frightening, unless you are wearing a lifejacket and are in the company of trusted swimmers. There is no certainty as to where the bottom might be. If as a beginner you were taken by boat to the deepest part of the lake and dropped off to swim to shore, the uncertain depth of the water below you would likely result in considerable anxiety ("dis-ease"). And if for some reason you were in the middle of an ocean, unable to see the shore, not knowing how deep the water was, or what might be swimming beneath you, you would likely be very anxious. If you were able to return to the shallow end of the pool or to the lakeshore, your anxiety would subside and linger only in your memory. The more extreme experience in the ocean, however, might result in a long-lasting fear of water. This type of fear can generally be ignored, although it is likely to recur if you ever find yourself in a similar situation. It can also be confronted. After all, it was not only the distance from the shore, the depth of the water, or the creatures of the sea that resulted in this fear. It was also the inability to swim, and the absence of other swimmers, lifejackets, boats, and navigation equipment.

This fear can be addressed by learning to swim, by understanding the ocean, by using a buddy system if you ever venture out again. Addressing the fear could also include training in navigation on the ocean and education about sea creatures. As you mature in your ability to swim and come to understand what it means to exist in the deep end, so to speak, the uncertainty is diminished, and anxiety decreases. The very place you feared most can even become a welcome challenge as you test your skills. Eventually it might become a place of enjoyment, associated with fond memories of the challenge you met head-on. But that cannot happen without facing the fear.

For many people, learning that they have a terminal illness is akin to the bottom falling out, of being in deep water, uncertain as to how you will get to shore, a shore that is not visible. For them, anxiety and fear are part of the experience. Again, anxiety and fear are normal features of life. You are more important than anything you fear or feel anxious about! Hopefully that notion will give you courage in the days, weeks, and months ahead as you look into the experience of living with a terminal illness.

In the context of having a terminal illness, what is your

anxiety about? Simply naming the anxiety may already diminish its effect. Finish the following sentence:

In the context of having a terminal illness, I feel anxious because . . .

....

....

....

....

Does your anxiety pertain to physical features of the illness experience? Are you anxious about the disease process? the symptoms that you are experiencing or that you might experience? the possibility of pain? Do you know anyone else who has had a similar illness?

....

....

....

....

Does your anxiety pertain to psychological features of the illness experience? How is this experience affecting your sense of self or who you are as a person? How might the experience affect your relationship with other people, especially those who are important to you?

....

....

....

....

....

Does your anxiety pertain to spiritual features of the illness experience? For some people, that might have to do with feeling betrayed by God, wondering about life after death, about reincarnation, or whether the teachings of their childhood are true. For others it may have to do with the uncertainty of the immediate and distant future.

_____

_____

_____

_____

_____

The issues and concerns mentioned above will be addressed in other sections of this manual. You may choose to speak with someone about your anxieties. In some instances a health-care provider, counselor or spiritual leader might be of great value with regard to exploring the source of your anxieties and different ways of addressing them.

Some people find relief from their anxiety by confronting it. Others might prefer to compartmentalize that part of themselves. In order to do that, imagine that your anxiety can be contained. How large is the container? What is its shape, weight, color? Imagine placing all your anxiety into the container. Then close the container, wrap it up, and tuck it away. You may choose to address the anxiety at another time.

Ambivalence

Ambivalence, that is, the simultaneous reality of opposites, may add to the anxiety:

- Are these symptoms real, or are they a feature of my imagination?
- Am I sick?
- Will I ever be well again?
- Is there medication available for this disease?
- Will the medication work?
- Am I living my life or am I dying?
- Do I continue working or do I resign?
- Do I tell someone how I really feel or do I contain my anxiety and fear in silence?
- Do I embrace life or do I prepare to die?

The ambivalence may be even greater if someone has a terminal illness and is taking medication or receiving treatment that *might* potentially reverse the disease process or lead to remission.

When I began my study, AIDS was regarded as a terminal illness. Every participant in the study who had been diagnosed with AIDS had been informed that he would likely die within six to twelve months. During the study, medications became available that changed the course of the disease. When the AIDS patients took the medication, what's known as the "viral load"—that is, the amount of virus in the body—decreased and the ability of the immune system to fight infections increased. As the prognosis changed from that of being a terminal illness with life expectancy of months to the possibility of being a chronic disease with a life expectancy of years, people's level of ambivalence seemed to increase.

- Does the disease raise issues of life and death, or of quality of life?
- Are the effects of the medication the same for everyone?
- Is it in my best interest to see this as a terminal illness or as a chronic disease?

This is similar to the ambivalence experienced by people with cancer who have been told that the disease they carry usually results in death but that with a new research drug the disease process might be reversed. Do these people prepare to die, or do they embrace living?

Bob had AIDS. He was very familiar with the disease, as a number of his friends and his partner of six years had died of AIDS. Bob lost his hearing in one ear and experienced the usual series of infections associated with the illness. He spoke of the ambivalence that filled his life:

> I look at myself in two ways. The one way is taking the pills, and the other way is not taking them. There's no cure around the corner. What's the point of taking all these pills for another fifteen or twenty years, or however long I'm around, and then having to do my intravenous [IV] medication every day? Cramming all these pills into my body, doing the IV, that just doesn't make sense to me—to have to do all that just to keep living. I'm not going to have the quality of life that I think I should have.

The medication and the IV served as a lifeline for Bob. But because he couldn't skip a day, he also experienced them as a ball and chain. The prognosis, that is the outcome, was unknown and uncertain.

> I don't know what to think, even the doctors don't really know. What should I plan for? Everyone I talk to, my nurse, my doctor, they seem confident that I'm going to get sick and die. Well, I don't feel like I'm sick, and because I'm not feeling sick, it makes me question whether I'm dying. It's really confusing. Maybe if I stopped eating so well it would weaken my system and I'd die quicker. It's just really bizarre to me. When I start thinking about life and some of the good things about life, I get worried. And there's the whole financial thing. I get a certain amount of money each month for ten years. What if I live beyond that point? Then I'll be in the poorhouse; what fun is that? When that money stops coming in, there's no way I'd be able to afford anything on what I make. And all those years lost in contributing to a retirement savings plan. All this stuff comes at you. *It's awful. I don't know which is better—life or death.*

When you have a terminal illness, it is difficult to know where you might be on the trajectory of life from birth to death. What are the indications that someone is dying? Is it in the lab results, personal appearance, the doctor's opinion, the amount of energy you have, your dreams and aspirations? It is difficult to know whether to pursue living and life or to prepare for dying and death. As Bob relates,

FACING DEATH, EMBRACING LIFE

The lab values pertaining to my immune system improved. On the one hand I'm happy, but on the other hand, I don't know. It makes me feel like I'm fine, and maybe I'll even go back to work. It makes you look at your life on a bigger scale.

Bob also spoke about the ambivalence he experienced:

I feel like I'm going crazy. I just really feel the need to go somewhere, anywhere. I want to take a chance and experience something new and different. I want to go and have an adventure in my life instead of sitting around this apartment all day popping pills every few hours. I feel like I'm in a no-win situation and that I've been that way for years. I'm sick of it. While I might be dying, I want to live to the fullest capacity I can. I want to go on an adventure with an open mind, an open spirit, an open heart and just make the best of what I can do. But I'm afraid that I'll get into some kind of trouble without anyone around to help me get through it. I might get mugged in the airport or something like that. I don't feel strong enough to go out and do something for myself because I have this disease. I have to take care of myself. Traveling can take a lot of energy out of you and wear you out while you're there. Then you'll get sick and you won't have anywhere to go. You'll be all alone. It would just be awful.

I don't know how much time I have, and this is something I've been wanting to do since I was in high school. I have a bit of money left; I'm in relatively stable health. My doctor has always told me, "You should go when you're having a stable period because if you wait until you're sick, you won't go." I just want to be at peace with myself. I want to do things and learn, and do as much as I can in the years I have, in the days that I have left.

Like anxiety, ambivalence is a normal and natural part of life and certainly is a normal and natural part of living with a terminal illness.

I feel ambivalent about

....

....

In order to move from ambivalence to action I would need

....

....

....

Death Anxiety

Ours is a time-conscious society. Ours is also a death-denying society. We search for immortality—in diets, exercise programs, plastic surgery to keep us looking youthful, treatments to cure incurable diseases. Through your experience of having a life-threatening disease, you become aware of death. It is important to continue living, yet death—and your anxiety about it—can no longer be ignored. It is not happening to the world outside you, to someone else. It is happening to you.

When we try to live up to the expectations of others— our family of origin, our family of choice, our culture, our memberships, our employers—we compromise our authenticity. In fact, we may be estranged from who we really are and what we would really like to do. This results in anxiety. Perhaps this is the anxiety at the core of all anxiety, that is, the anxiety of *not living the life we would truly like to live*. Certainly it contributes to death anxiety. In that sense, it would seem that death anxiety is related to life anxiety.

- If I am living in a way that is true to myself, would I fear death?
- And if I fear death, am I really living as I would like to be living?

- If I lived my life without trying to meet the expectations of anyone else, who would I be, and how would I live?

- If I knew that my life would be coming to an end within a specific amount of time, how would I live today?

To ask those questions—and to answer them—is to experience both components of time: measured time and soulful time. Some people's lives are consumed by such questions. They struggle for the answers. For them, that struggle results in ambivalence and anxiety.

In writing about death anxiety, Dr. Irvin Yalom, a psychiatrist working with people who have cancer, cites the work of James Diggory and Doreen Rothman. Those two researchers asked more than 550 people in the general population to place seven consequences of death in order of importance. The people who responded to the questionnaire reported that their number-one concern was the grief their death would cause relatives and friends. I have found that this deep anxiety about the effect of your own death on the people you love may keep you from speaking about that fear or speaking about your own fears regarding death. It may add to a sense of isolation, of aloneness. For some people, the need to take care of others is greater than their desire to alleviate their own fear and anxiety by speaking about those emotions.

According to Diggory, the respondents' greatest fear about death as it affected their own individual lives was that all their plans and projects would come to an end and that they could no longer have any experiences. They also mentioned fear of pain in the process of dying, an inability to care for dependents, and fear of what might happen to them if there was life after death.

Death anxiety has to do with the fear of "not being," of annihilation. Yalom also cites the work of Kierkegaard. Yalom explains that Kierkegaard was the first to distinguish between fear and anxiety, that is, fear and dread. Fear of *something* differs from fear of "no thing," the latter being identified as dread.

"One dreads (or is anxious about) losing oneself and becoming nothingness." This anxiety is not specific, it is a generalized sense of dread. A fear that is not specific and cannot be understood "becomes more terrible still: it begets a feeling of helplessness which invariably generates further anxiety." In this way, fear that is not specific becomes anxiety. How, then, can we address death anxiety? Again, as Yalom writes, "If we can transform fear of nothing to a fear of something, we can mount some self-protective campaign—that is, we can either avoid the thing we fear, seek allies against it, develop magical rituals to placate it, or plan a systematic campaign to detoxify it."

Although death cannot be avoided, most people consciously avoid thoughts of death. Many live in denial of the reality of death. It is more difficult to avoid or ignore death once you receive the diagnosis of a terminal illness. Knowing that you have a limited amount of time remaining, you are challenged to face death and embrace living. You find yourself asking, *Have I lived the life I have always wanted to live?* The degree to which you are able to answer in the positive will likely affect the degree of anxiety you experience.

According to Yalom, the attributes of death anxiety include concern for others, fear of premortal pain and postmortal (life after death) possibilities, and annihilation, that is, "not being." This is the emotion we experience when we stop to think and feel who we are when the clock stops, when time as we know it ends. Who are we then? We are no longer who we thought we were. Knowing that we will cease to be, becomes part of our new reality. That realization results in a universal anxiety. It is an emotion without boundaries, like floating in a limitless ocean, with no horizon in sight.

Consider first your concern for others, in the context of no longer being here for them. Who are the people you are most concerned about?

....

....

....

What roles do you play in their lives? What roles do they play in your life? Are they dependent on you in any way? If so, how? How do you contribute to their well-being?

....

....

....

....

....

....

How will their lives be different when you are no longer physically present? What have you given them, in terms of your relationship, that will be with them after you die?

....

....

....

....

....

....

....

....

One of the most difficult questions to ask and to think about is: What will the world be like when I am no longer in it? Where will I be? What will happen to me? Much as the swimmer requires assistance and new resources when learning to swim in the deep end, anyone facing a terminal illness would do well to seek resources to help address the fear and anxiety resulting from the diagnosis. We can speak to experts about pain management; we can speak to those we love about our sadness at leaving them and the grief they will experience after we have died; we can make arrangements to address the financial, emotional, and spiritual burdens or well-being of those who are dependent on us; and perhaps we can gain perspective on questions of life after death from religious leaders and from those who have had near-death experiences. These are all important strategies that will help reduce the anxiety. However, there is still cause for significant anxiety, namely, that no one returns from annihilation, from "not being." Can the anxiety be altered or significantly reduced? Can the experience of dying be otherwise?

It can be so, but only by asking the questions that directly pertain to our anxiety. The anxiety must be translated into a fear, for fear can be met with courage. Begin by asking yourself, What is it about this anxiety that can be identified as a fear? Name the fears. The first step to getting rid of the fear is to say it aloud:

I am afraid. I am afraid of the disease within me. I am afraid of dying. I am afraid to tell you how fearful I am. I am afraid to let you know that I know I am very sick. I am afraid of speaking about my fears. I am afraid of how those around me will cope if I say out loud what I am experiencing on the inside. I am afraid that I won't have the courage to do and say what needs to be done and said. I don't want to die. I don't want to suffer. I need courage to face my dying. If I have all this fear, what does that say about my present existence? About my faith or my religious tradition? What does that say about who I am, who I have been, and who I want to be?

In this context some people confront the fear by acknowledging that they are not living the life they would like to live, not being in relationships the way they would like to be, not experiencing spirituality in a way that is meaningful to them. On a profound level, these people ask themselves, *Who am I?* They speak their own truth and listen to the truth of those who are dear to them. They seek and find meaning in the transcendent.

In the midst of all the anxiety that is present when someone has a terminal illness, the focus of that person and those who love them is often placed on finding a cure, finding the doctor who knows the most about a particular disease process or treatment, or traveling to another country for an intervention. The search and the response to what they find consumes time and energy. People begin to live in response to the wishes of others because the real issues are too difficult to speak about. Children beg parents to try an alternate treatment, families ask that physicians persuade a family member to try one more course of therapy, people pool financial resources to send someone to another country for a second opinion or a particular intervention. All of those actions are legitimate. But too often they take the place of strengthening relationships, of enhancing intimacy, or of sharing important features of one

FACING DEATH, EMBRACING LIFE

another's life stories. Sometimes they impede honest and open conversations on topics that are difficult to raise. Some of those topics will be discussed in the next chapters.

TWO

Bad News

When did you last receive bad news, or life-altering news? How did you learn about it? What effect did it have on you? Would the effect have been different if you had been informed in another way?

....

....

....

....

....

....

Receiving bad news is never easy, and giving bad news is one of the great challenges inherent in being a physician. Informing someone that they have a terminal illness is not a technical skill but rather a communication skill that calls for all the wisdom and compassion the doctor has to offer.

For some of us the end of life will come sooner than we hoped or expected. We may discover that we have a terminal illness such as AIDS, cancer or ALS, or that there is no known cure for the disease process going on within us. We may also be informed that the disease we have been living with for many years is no longer reversible, as might be the case in congestive heart failure, chronic obstructive lung disease, or pulmonary fibrosis. In those instances, life, dying and death take on a new reality.

In most cases, we learn about having a terminal illness from a physician. There are many physicians who have strong communication skills, making them very effective in the work they do. However, there are others who—without even being aware of it—cause people to suffer by not communicating in a compassionate manner.

If you have been told by a physician that you have a terminal illness, it is possible that you felt hurt through that experience. Although I'm certain that it was the intent of the doctor to provide comprehensive, compassionate care and not to add to your suffering, all too often that particular encounter does cause suffering. You may have a memory of a painful experience among your encounters with physicians or interactions with other health-care providers. The fact that this might be a part of the experience of living with a terminal illness became very apparent through a research project I conducted that involved having conversations with people who had been informed that they had a terminal illness. It was a disconcerting realization. I learned that despite all the good that is done in the context of medical practice, poor communication can render ineffective all the good intentions in medicine, as it has the potential to increase suffering. If you have received a message from a physician that was delivered in a way that caused suffering, your relationship with that physician is likely different than it was before you received the message. That may be the case even if there was no intent to cause you suffering. In fact, in most instances it is the physician's desire to do good in your life. However, the messages we receive from others may affect our relationships with those people simply because of the way they are delivered.

The strongest and most intimate relationships we can have are those in which we feel safe and are able to trust one another. In safety and trust, people are able to speak honestly about who they are and about their hopes, desires, expectations and needs. In that context, people are also able to speak about fears, anxieties, failures and concerns. One would hope that those features would characterize the doctor/patient relationship at a time when information regarding a terminal illness is given.

Communication is one of humanity's greatest accomplishments. It is the cornerstone, the foundation, of all our relationships. Communication is part of every human interaction, affecting those we work with, those we serve, and those we love. Communication has verbal and nonverbal features. Most of what we communicate is nonverbal. In fact, up to eighty percent of the message we give to others is given through nonverbal communication, that is, through features such as tone of voice, gestures, posture, facial expressions and the physical distance between two people.

Think of the way you communicate at work and at home. Remember an incident where you and the person you were speaking with seemed not to understand each other. What was it that you were trying to communicate? How was it received? How was it misunderstood? Thinking back, what were your

intentions and what effect did they have on the other person?
What assumptions were each of you making? Did you stop to
ask questions about the difficulty you experienced in communicating? What might you have done differently?

At times, when we communicate, our best intentions may have
tragic consequences, while at other times the outcome may
have a neutral or a healing effect. What we hope to accomplish
may not always come to pass. One of the basic problems in our
relationships, either personal or professional, has to do with the
difference between what one person intends to communicate
and how another person actually hears and receives the
message. Whenever we communicate with another person, we
assume that our intentions will lead to the desired outcome.
We don't often ask the other person for a response to the effect
of a particular communication. It seems that the more intimate
the relationship, the greater the likelihood of making assumptions. At times the intent and the effect may be very congruent.
At other times the two may be opposite to one another. The
degree of congruence between the message given and the message received is known, as first described by John Wallen, as the
interpersonal gap. Much of who we are is embedded in every
message we communicate to others. In turn, much of who they
are is embedded in their translation of the message we are
giving to them. The nonverbal component of communication

adds to the complexity of the interaction, as we may not be aware of many of the features of our own nonverbal communication. These features comprise a large part of the message and are there to be translated by those who receive our messages.

Communication is significant in every doctor/patient relationship. Because the information exchange has to do with one's health and well-being, it is especially important. And, like any other interaction, the communication itself may have a healing effect or, in some instances, a harming effect.

The interpersonal gap is always present in our personal conversations, as well as in our work-related or professional conversations. It has to do with intent, effect and assumptions. Consider the story of Max.

Max was a man in his late twenties, a graduate student who also worked on computer systems for a transport company. Because Max had been diagnosed with diabetes during his adolescent years, he was very familiar with the health-care system. He understood the disease process and knew how to manage it. Four years after the initial diagnosis, the symptoms of his disease seemed to flare up again. He felt overwhelming fatigue and at times experienced some abdominal discomfort. The doctor he visited at the time attributed his symptoms, not to the diabetes, but to stress. He suggested that Max alter his lifestyle. Instead, Max chose to maintain his lifestyle and to tolerate the pain and discomfort, until one day, two years later, he collapsed at work.

> I went to see a doctor the next day, thinking that I'd stop in before work, and that everything would be hunky-dory. This was a different doctor! He took my claims seriously. When I started talking about night sweats and not

being able to sleep and having to take lots of Tylenol, it immediately sent bells off in his mind. He palpated my stomach and immediately said, "We want to admit you to the hospital. We need to run some ultrasound tests." "Whoa, slow down! Admit? Don't you only do that for people who are seriously ill?" He looked at me and said, "This is definitely not your imagination. There is something going on in there. It's involving at least your spleen and your liver."

This doctor took Max very seriously. He did not trivialize the symptoms nor the information regarding Max's inability to function at work, the changes in his relationships with his friends, or the loss of concentration that was affecting his academic performance.

So on the one hand, I was extremely freaked that this sort of diagnosis was dropped in my lap. On the other hand, I was relieved. I was finally gonna get some answers. I spent about two weeks in the hospital. The entire time I was there, they sort of danced around the issue. You know . . . *what is it?* "It could be anything. What we know for sure is that there is a mass in your lower pelvic region and we'll know more once we do more tests." Well, more tests were done, and my condition deteriorated quite rapidly. Doctors are running around doing all kinds of tests that I've never heard of—needle biopsies and all kinds of things. And then a surgeon comes up and says that he wants to perform an open biopsy, a laparotomy. I was hesitant but decided to go ahead with it. After the open biopsy was performed, I waited and waited. Days are clicking by. This is very stressful, not only for me but for my whole family.

I got tired of waiting. I knew when the nurses would be on rounds and away from the nurses' station. I went to the nurses' station and pulled my chart, opened it up, looked under diagnosis, and there it was: metastatic carcinoma. That meant nothing to me, so I wrote it down on a little piece of paper. When the nurse came in to do the vitals, I said, "Do you have a medical dictionary? I'm curious to look up a few terms." She brought the dictionary, and I flipped right to "carcinoma," which it turns out means cancer. So then I looked up the word "metastatic," which means something that has spread. I wrote that down: "spread cancer." I finally had some idea of what was going on.

In time Max was transferred to another institution. He was not pleased about the transfer.

I didn't like it and made this fact known. The admitting nurse turned to me and said, "Well, what do you expect, this isn't the Westin Bayshore Hotel."

(The Westin Bayshore Hotel is one of Vancouver's upscale waterfront hotels.)

If I could have one more hour with any of the people who participated in the research project, the person I would choose would be Max. I still hear the wincing in Max's voice, I see the anguish in his face. I wish for Max's sake that someone at the hospital would have greeted him with compassion, empathy, and understanding; that someone had held him, touched his shoulder, or placed a hand on his hand; that someone had addressed the anxiety, the fear, the uncertainty he was experiencing. I also wish that I had demonstrated those same features as I listened to his story. I didn't meet him with compassion and empathy either. I simply sat listening to his story, experiencing some doubt and disbelief within myself. In my mind, I trivialized his reality by assuming that he was simply experiencing the natural stages of grief and terminal illness. Rather than understanding the story from his perspective I assumed he was in the angry stage of his experience. That was easy to understand. I would be angry too if I was in my early twenties and had been told that I would die within two years. Max did not intend for me to sympathize with him, he only wanted me to understand his experience from his perspective, not from my place of knowledge and life experience. But, as much as I wanted Max's experience to be the exception with regard to the research I was doing, I now know that was not the case.

I made an incorrect assumption. I assumed that Max was angry because of the disease process going on within him. I also assumed he had misunderstood the physicians, that they could not possibly have interacted with him in the way he described. I was no different than the physician he visited after the initial pain and fatigue he was experiencing. The interpersonal gap between us was significant. I misunderstood Max. It is my sense that his message did not have the intended effect until some time later, when I met others with similar stories.

Max continued:

The physician came in and rattled off a big pathological name and told me that I was going to die in two to two-and-a-half years. In the span of about two minutes he took away all my hopes and dreams. At that point, I felt like suicide was a viable option.

Think of the concept of the interpersonal gap in this instance. I am certain that the physician was intending to be truthful about the diagnosis and about giving information to Max that he needed to have. The effect was one of despair and isolation, leading to suicidal ideation. The conversation was one of extreme incongruence and a very large interpersonal gap, one that resulted in great suffering. That suffering was still present and apparent at the time that I heard Max's story several years later. Perhaps, for whatever reason, both Max and the physician were suffering.

I know now that my attitude toward Max at the time he was telling me his story was not one of empathy. When Max spoke those words, I could hardly believe him. I don't believe I fully understood or appreciated what it was that he was saying. I wanted to find an explanation for his experience that was less incriminating. I really was no different than the people he was describing. If I had another opportunity to spend time with Max I would work hard to understand his story from his perspective. I would ask him how the doctors might have been sensitive to who he was, how he would have wanted to receive the information about his new diagnosis and how I as a physician could be compassionate toward him.

You may have your own examples of when a doctor, nurse or other health-care provider spoke to you or your loved one, or was silent, in a way that added to your suffering, despair, frustration and anger. Those who describe the experience usually do so with a degree of anger and disbelief, a real sense of betrayal, regardless of how much time has passed since their experience. Betrayal in a relationship usually means there is a loss of trust, which is an essential ingredient in the doctor/patient relationship. It is difficult to have a meaningful relationship without trust.

Describe the scenario in which trust between you and a health-care provider was broken.

_____

_____

_____

_____

_____

_____

_____

When my physician gave me information I did not want (for example, your cholesterol is still dangerously high despite your change in diet and the exercise you have been doing; your pregnancy test is negative again; you have signs of early dementia; all the signs and symptoms point to cancer) I felt

_____

_____

_____

The specific message I got was

_____

_____

_____

What I needed my physician to say at that time was

....

....

....

....

What I need my physician to hear is

....

....

....

....

In order for trust to be re-established I would need my physician to say or do the following:

....

....

....

....

....

Max did have a positive experience with some nurses, while others added to his suffering. "Some nurses were absolute dolls. Others, well, maybe I'm asking, 'Please don't use that vein.' They come back with something like, 'I've been doing this for seventeen years, and who do you think you are trying to order me around.' And they just go ahead. Nobody deserves to be treated like that. It's not fair to the patient or to the patient's family."

Max was right. It isn't fair that a person should have to suffer because of a physician's insensitivity or a nurse's impatience. To do good and not to do harm is as important a feature of communication as it is a feature of interventions that reverse disease processes.

Some people have a very different experience from Max. For them, the interpersonal gap is much smaller. Peggy is such a person.

Peggy, a fine-featured woman in her late sixties, lay quietly in her hospital bed. With her eyes closed, Peggy recalled how, after coming up the stairs from the basement, she found herself gasping for breath, alone in her kitchen, wishing she could die, believing she would die, when her daughter Kathy dropped by on her way home from work. Thank God Kathy got there when she did and called for an ambulance! Today, for the second time since her admission to the hospital, the draining of fluid from around her lungs had given Peggy "new breath." She remembered a time in her life when her physical activity had not been compromised by lack of energy or shortness of breath, when she was able to take long walks along Jericho Beach—her dog, Duke, beside her, the mountains in clear view across English Bay. Remembering those walks seemed to give her a certain calmness, a deep sense that an inner strength would sustain her through anything.

Peggy's memories and thoughts were interrupted by a gentle touch on her right arm. It was Dr. Neilson. He spoke with her about draining the fluid from her chest cavity, of injecting a substance to prevent the fluid from collecting again, and of what she might expect in the days and weeks ahead.

The first question I always asked my co-researchers (the people who participated in the research project) was how they learned about their illness, either the initial diagnosis or the point at which they were told that it was not curable, that in fact it was a terminal illness, one that would likely be the cause of their death. All of them described the situation in considerable detail. Some of them remembered exactly how it had happened even though it had occurred years earlier.

Peggy replied:

I've been very, very fortunate with the medical care I've received. I guess the first thing to tell you is that I trust all my physicians. They've been totally up front and answered questions in detail. I have a daughter who's very involved in the medical field, and she has sat in on all the important interviews and has asked questions that have clarified things in their minds, too. So in my case, I couldn't have asked for it to be handled better because everybody has been so up front with me, told me what it might be, what it might not be. I mean they just couldn't have been more honest, so it didn't come as a shock, a bolt out of the blue at all. It was just one of the case scenarios they described that they hoped it wouldn't be.

I asked Peggy to be specific about the interactions between her doctor and herself with her family. Her response:

What is particularly in my mind is the day my youngest flew in from Cleveland, Ohio. It was the first time Dr. Neilson had seen all three girls together. I asked him to go over my history with them because the way things happened was a little confusing to them. He did it very succinctly but with a lot of empathy, touching me from time to time while he was talking to them. My youngest lost her cool. She got up and left the room. He finished talking to the other two and left, and then one of my girls went to find their younger sister. They found her in the lounge. Dr. Neilson was there with her, his arm around her, comforting her. I feel an aura of spirituality around him. He would never lie to any of us or fudge the truth on anything. There have been occasions when he could have "soft soaped" anything. He didn't, but then obviously he's got a clear sense of how much we could take.

I wish Peggy's experience was typical. I wish it was the norm. In this instance, it seems that there was congruence between the intent of the physician and the effect his message had on Peggy. The interpersonal gap was small. Unfortunately, that is not always the case. Physicians and health-care providers often forget that hearing bad news can result in anger—at change, at the information itself, at life, illness, mortality, and, finally, at the messenger. How the message is given can affect the emotional response. Thus one must ask, What is the best way of giving and receiving the kind of information that is difficult to hear? Many medical schools and medical post-graduate training programs include training in communication skills to prepare physicians to give information in a respectful, factual and compassionate manner.

In my research, a portion of the suffering that people experienced resulted from the way doctors had communicated with them. It also resulted from their interactions with other health-care providers. Although the doctor makes the diagnosis and breaks the news to the patient, many other health-care professionals are involved in providing care during a hospital stay. For some of my co-researchers, interactions with these professionals added to their suffering; for others, they engendered a sense of trust and safety.

People working in health care are familiar with their environment, their jobs, and their responsibilities. But some forget that your admission to the hospital might be your first, and they assume that you are as familiar with things as they are. If this happens, you should express concerns, ask questions, work to participate in the decision-making regarding your care. I know this is difficult when you are tired, experiencing discomfort or pain, and feeling vulnerable because of your dependence on others. You might find it easier if you ask family and friends for support in getting the information and the interaction you need. If that is the case, you might ask the doctor when he plans to see you the next day. Let the doctor know that you are asking that question because one of your family members or friends would like to be present. You could also ask one of the nurses to check with the doctor as to the time of his next visit. Many doctors regularly make rounds before or after their office work. Other staff members might know that about specific doctors and be able to suggest a time for your family member to be present.

Once in a meeting with the doctor, ask about your diagnosis, the treatment options, what would happen if you choose not to follow the treatment options, medications—their desired effects and their side effects—and your expected time of discharge.

While I seemed unable to hear Max, Marjorie got my attention.

Marjorie was a pleasant, articulate, silver-haired woman in her mid-seventies. During my first visit with her, I asked how she had learned about her diagnosis. She told me about discovering the lump in her left groin and about the events that followed: the visit to her family doctor, the consultation with a specialist, then waiting for months while the lump grew to the size deemed necessary for excision. She was assured that the growth was likely benign. This process of investigation, diagnosis and treatment had happened ten years before Marjorie told me about it, but she remembered the details of the events as though they had happened the day before our initial time together.

> I was still in the hospital. This part is the first trauma. Up to then I don't remember any great emotion. I was lying in my bed, still coming out of the anesthesia, and the doctor appeared at the door. Without coming into the room, he told me, "We were wrong. It's cancer."
>
> No, he didn't say cancer. He said, "It's metastatic carcinoma." Normally I would know what that was, but I was dazed and I said, "What's that mean?" He said, "It means you have cancer. Don't worry, I'll make an appointment for you at the cancer clinic." He never came in. He spoke to me from the door and then left.

She felt hurt and very angry.

Marjorie was told she could go home the next morning. She spent the night weeping, not because she had learned that she had cancer but because of the *way* she learned about it. Although she didn't think of herself as a very assertive person, she decided she would not go home until she had spoken with her doctor. In the morning, he appeared at the door again, and she asked him to come in.

> He said, "What's the matter? You can go home now." I said, "I have to tell you something." He said, "Well, what

is it?" And I said, "It's the way you told me I have cancer. You've known me for more than three months. I thought that you considered me a person, not just a disease, but then you stood in the door and told me I had cancer and went away." He said, "What should I have done?" I said, "Well, you could have come in and put your hand on my shoulder and then told me I have cancer. It would have made a big difference to me. You don't have to say, 'Oh, you poor thing!' Just say, 'You've got cancer, and we're going to take care of it.'"

Looking back over the ten years since that diagnosis, Marjorie said that the emotional pain she experienced was greater than any of the physical pain she experienced. She was unable to forget her memory of that experience.

When Marjorie confronted her doctor about her emotional pain after his rather evasive demeanor, he said, "Because of the work I do regarding women with breast cancer, I have to tell so many women this. That's the only way I can do it." I am certain that he had no intention of hurting her; he seemed not to realize that he could have spared her much suffering if only he had come into the room, sat next to her and had spoken with compassion.

Experiencing pain because of a bad interaction with a health-care provider isn't uncommon. Don't be afraid to do what you think is right in that regard: communicate person to person, write a letter, or phone from home. Explain your point of view, identify your preferred outcome, and relay your preferences for the future. This is your experience, your illness, your life. If the pain is too great and you have lost your sense of trust in the doctor, then it might be time to find another doctor.

Some doctors may feel that the moment they break the bad news about a terminal illness is the point at which they have nothing more to offer. On the contrary, they can commit to being there for the patient regardless of the outcome of treatment, to control pain and manage other symptoms, to support family and friends. This may be the time of greatest need for the patient. It is when the focus shifts to prolongation of life, quality of life, pain control, symptom management, and issues that contribute to suffering—physically, psychologically and spiritually. Suffering is diminished when those who suffer are understood. For your own benefit, ask your attending physician what you might expect from him/her (either or both pronouns will be used throughout this manual) during the course of your illness.

I often receive phone calls from friends and acquaintances asking how to communicate with physicians, how to get the information they need and want. The practice of medicine is changing for many reasons. Time is of the essence. Being efficient during the visit with the doctor is of benefit to the physician. Your relationship with the doctors that provide care for you is very important. Understanding that relationship might be important to your sense of well-being. Below, I have included some features that might enhance that understanding.

Suppose you are visiting a doctor because of a symptom that is causing you concern, a symptom that has disrupted your life. The doctor thinks of that symptom in terms of a disease process and seeks to understand it more fully through hearing your story, by conducting a physical examination, making clinical observations and by running tests (blood work, urine samples, X–rays, CT scans, etc.). The doctor will focus on the body system pertaining to the concern that you bring. That is what is expected of the physician.

Consider your visit to the doctor.

1. If you have more than one medical/health issue to discuss, write them down in order of priority before you visit the doctor's office. Mention at the beginning of your visit that you have several concerns, and that you would like to discuss the first two or three if time permits.

Health Concerns (in order of priority):

1. ....
2. ....
3. ....
4. ....
5. ....

Ask how much time the doctor has allowed for your visit. The schedules of most family physicians are based on ten- to fifteen-minute visits. It might even be less than that. Apart from the time that the doctor spends with you, she will also need time for charting, that is, entering a note about your visit on the chart, either a paper chart or an electronic chart, getting the office assistant to make appointments, contacting specialists by phone, referral form or by letter.

If only two concerns are addressed in the allotted time, inform the doctor of the third so that she can assess its urgency. Keep in mind that if your doctor spends an extra ten minutes on every patient, the waiting room will soon fill up with impatient people. So, let her know that you would be pleased to make another appointment if necessary. If you work within the system as it is today, your relationship with the doctor will likely be a positive one. If you want to speak with the doctor for a longer period of time, ask whether she has any time set aside for longer visits in the course of a week when she might simply speak to you about your concern. For example, some doctors keep one or two appointment times for "counseling" at the end of the morning or at the end of the day.

2. Give the doctor as much specific information as you can for each symptom. Changes in regular function (e.g., sleep, appetite, weight, bowel and bladder function, libido) are noteworthy. Describe the experience of the symptom—when it started, how it has changed over time, what makes it better or worse. If you feel a burning sensation in your stomach during a nap, don't just say, "I think I have an ulcer" (feel free to add your personal diagnosis after describing the symptoms, especially if you've been treated for similar symptoms before). In your description, include any treatment you tried at home (including alternative treatments—don't be apprehensive about that); name any and all the medications you used; and by all means, inform the doctor whether you've seen another health-care professional about this. If you feel awkward about something you did, then say so: "I feel awkward saying this, but I want you to know that . . ."

What is your reason for seeing the doctor?

a. What is the symptom? Has it occurred before? How often and under what circumstances? What made you decide to visit the physician about this concern at this time?

....
....
....

b. Where do you feel the symptom?

....
....
....

c. When do you feel the symptom?

....
....
....

d. How did it start? How has it changed over time?

....
....
....

e. What makes it better or worse?

....
....
....

f. Inform the doctor about the treatments you have tried.

....
....
....

g. Inform the doctor about other health-care professionals you have seen regarding this health concern.

....

....

....

h. Tell the doctor what you fear most about this symptom. That might include information about a family member or a friend who had a similar symptom. Or it might simply be your own fear of what this symptom means to you.

....

....

....

....

3. Once the doctor makes her decision about the disease process, she will speak to you about the diagnosis and treatment. The doctor may also recommend tests. Be sure you understand their purpose, the process and the diagnosis. If you're anxious, fearful or upset in any way, tell the doctor. She may be able to clarify things in a way that reduces your fear. Knowing what to expect at the outset means you won't let your imagination run wild.

a. What is the test? What is the purpose of the test?

....

....

b. What information will the test give that you don't already have?

_____

_____

c. Is there a risk in having the test done? Might the test be painful or uncomfortable?

_____

_____

d. Other than confirming a diagnosis or giving added information about the disease process going on, will the test results change the treatment plan?

_____

_____

e. How long will it take for the test results to be known after the test is done?

_____

_____

f. How will the doctor inform you of the test results? E.g., by phone call, office visit, invitation to come in given by receptionist?

_____

_____

4. How would you like to hear news that will likely change your life, such as the diagnosis of a terminal illness?

_____

_____

Some doctors, especially those who know their patients well, choose to give information in small doses, knowing that the patient will get the bigger picture in due course. Other doctors hold back for fear they will increase their patient's anxiety. Asking for information or stating that you would like to know as much as possible will help the doctor to determine how best to give you the information you need at that time. Ask questions until you understand the disease process, the treatment options, and the expected outcomes. You could say things like, "If I understand you correctly, what is happening is . . ." Remember that many people have difficulty "hearing" any information that follows the diagnosis of a serious illness. You will likely need to hear the same information several times in order to assimilate it into your life. Work to understand the message. Take notes if you need to, or ask the doctor to write the diagnosis on a piece of paper. It might also be of benefit to write down the names of other doctors (including their specialties) you will be going to see and the times of your next appointments.

5. If the treatment includes medication, ask whether it is to be taken before or after meals, with or without food, when you might expect it to start working, the presence and severity of its side effects, and how long you will likely have to stay on it. Make certain that the doctor knows about other medications you are taking and whether you have prescriptions for them or not. Birth-control pills, medication for indigestion, and over-the-counter sleeping pills are often forgotten.

Again, take notes if necessary. Friends and family members will ask you a thousand questions if they know that you have been to see a doctor. A few notes may be valuable in answering those questions, not to mention keeping a record for yourself. The key words to remember are "truth," "touch," and "time." Ideally, your physician is able to speak the *truth, touch* you with compassion, and give the *time* that is necessary to bring you to a frank understanding of your situation while minimizing distress. If you have a serious illness, you want to know about all your options—surgical, radiation, chemotherapy. Are the interventions intended to reverse the disease process, that is, to cure you, or are they intended for palliation, that is, for your comfort?

6. If you sense that you're facing a life-threatening illness or news that a disease has progressed, bring along a friend or family member. Some people value the company, even for more mundane visits. Most people, even veteran health-care professionals, feel some anxiety when visiting a doctor. An extra set of ears could make a big difference. But if you do invite someone to join you (or if you yourself accompany a patient during a visit), consider the following suggestions. Go to the doctor's office together. Ask the doctor's permission in advance, take notes on the key information, and write out some questions before the visit. Some doctors may ask if you want the guest

present throughout the visit (including the examination) or whether you prefer that they start with you, leave during the examination, and return for the discussion. Some rooms might be very small, which might limit the presence of additional people, especially during the examination. Some people actually tape the discussion. Perhaps this is not necessary when hearing the bad news for the first time, but it might be helpful on subsequent visits when decisions are being made about treatment plans.

7. Make a follow-up appointment for test results, anticipating when they'll become available. Making the follow-up appointment at the time of the initial visit can reduce waiting time and the consequent anxiety.

8. Listen carefully to everything that is said. Ask questions. Have terms and concepts defined and clarified. Request copies of reports. Offer to pay for photocopying. Have the reports explained in layman's terms. Ask more questions. Advise the doctor that you'll want all the information that is known about the disease process (known as the natural history of the disease). Ask what you can expect in following a particular course of treatment (the protocol) and what you can expect if you choose not to have the treatment. How many patients has the doctor cared for using this particular treatment? What was their experience? What was the outcome? If surgery is recommended, how long will the recovery period be? How tired will you be through the recovery period? Will you have the energy to do the things you want to do? How much is the recovery period lengthened or made more difficult by the underlying disease process? If you decide not to

take a particular medication or have a recommended surgery, does that mean such options will forever be closed to you? And if you choose not to take these options, who will provide medical care as your disease progresses?

9. Tell the doctor that this information is valuable to you as well as to your family; you want as much control of your life as possible. There are things you still want to do, people you want to see, some inner preparation you may need to make. Ask permission to call back with other questions or requests. (But remember that doctors don't generally get paid for telephone conversations. For that reason, some doctors might prefer that you make another appointment. It's not that the doctor is only interested in money; she practices medicine, and seeing patients is how she earns a living.) It might be better to make an appointment to see the doctor again in a few days or weeks. It is usual for much of the information presented on that first visit not to be retained. That alone might be reason enough to see the doctor again.

You face many decisions once you have been told you have a terminal illness. It is crucial to remember that the choices belong to you, the patient, whether they pertain to the disease process, the treatment, or the life you want to live with

the time and energy you have remaining. In fact, the unfinished business, your sense of self, and your relationship with
others may be as important as (or even more important than)
focusing all your attention on the disease process.

Even in relationships where information is given in a
wise and compassionate manner, feeling hurt is a possibility,
but the probability is diminished. Your doctor may not be perfect, and he may have already made mistakes that have hurt
you. But you can work to create a better relationship with the
doctor that will help to minimize your anxiety and suffering. If
your efforts to do so are not met with equal effort in return, in
most communities you have the choice to move on and to create that relationship with another doctor. If there is not an
option to change doctors, it might be very important for you to
have a discussion with the physician about the communication between the two of you. The suffering you have experienced in that regard need not continue.

THREE

Physical Pain

Remember the last time you were in pain. What was that experience like? How did it start? How long did it last? How did it affect your work, your play, your hobbies, your ability to concentrate, your interest in the world around you, your relationship with other people? How did other people respond to you while you were in pain? What did you do to rid yourself of the pain?

FACING DEATH, EMBRACING LIFE

Now remember an experience of physical pain when you were a child. What did you learn about pain as a child?

_____

_____

_____

_____

How did your parents or siblings respond to you when you experienced pain as a child?

_____

_____

_____

How did you, as a child, respond to other people who experienced pain? How do you as an adult respond to the pain experienced by other people?

_____

_____

_____

_____

How do you respond to your own pain? How would you like others to respond to you when you are experiencing pain?

_____

_____

_____

_____

Every day millions of people experience pain. For a great percentage of them, pain is part of their illness. The pain can result from the disease itself, treatment (surgery, chemotherapy, radiation) or factors unrelated to the particular disease. Many people have more than one type of pain, each with a different cause and therefore perhaps a different treatment. Whatever the cause, however, the initial fear and anxiety experienced with an increase in pain or with the start of a new pain may be that the disease has progressed or recurred. Pain may or may not increase or change as the disease progresses, that is, the degree of pain does not necessarily correlate to progression of the disease. In fact, some people never experience pain as part of the disease process going on within them, while others experience a great deal of pain, even though they may not have "a lot of disease." Many people with a terminal illness receive the necessary care to control their pain and other symptoms, such that they are able to enjoy an optimal quality of life. For most, pain can be controlled. Unfortunately, in many cases pain that could be controlled is not.

Max, a diabetic for several years before being diagnosed as having cancer, experienced severe pain as a result of the cancer:

> I'm not sleeping at all and it's getting to the point where in the middle of the night four or five o'clock in the morning rolls around I'm tossing and turning from the pain and from the discomfort. And I'm just so exhausted, you know this has gone on for weeks on end and I fall asleep simply from sheer exhaustion, not from actually being able to fall asleep or anything like that. I was falling asleep with the pain and I was just thankful if I got forty minutes, fifty minutes, whatever the case might be.

Max spoke about the all-consuming effect of his pain. It affected his capacity to work, his relationships with his friends, his ability to sleep and his appetite. Max experienced pain for months. It affected his whole sense of being.

> The pain got more and more severe, and nothing seemed to relieve it. There was no position I could lie in or sit in that would relieve it. There was no analgesic or painkiller I could take that would alleviate it. It seemed to be related to my blood sugar, so I didn't look for another explanation. It got so bad that my sleep became fragmented, and this started to affect other areas of my life.
>
> This lack of sleep was affecting my studies and my ability to do my job. I got to the point where I couldn't go a night without it happening. I knew that, if my blood sugars went an iota above 10, I'd be in pain; so I'm having to keep tighter control on my blood sugars, which is increasingly difficult. It's starting to invade other areas of my life—my friendships, my relationship with my girlfriend. I started to do strange things. Since I'm not able to sleep, I would sit huddled up, watching TV and waiting for the insulin to take effect, to drop my blood sugars so that the pain would go away. I started to take excessive amounts of Tylenol because now the pain had entered my lower abdomen.

In time, pain commonly results in social isolation and withdrawal, depression, changes in ability to function, and sleep disturbances. At times Max was hesitant to speak to his parents about his pain because he did not want to burden them. This added to his sense of isolation and contributed to the anxiety he was experiencing.

People in pain are robbed of sleep, especially those people in severe pain. They, like Max, may steal a few hours of sleep at a time and even that sleep often leaves them feeling unrested, as tired as they were before they fell asleep. Max spoke of getting a bit of sleep whenever he could during the day because often the pain was so great at night that he was unable to sleep at all. In an effort to alleviate the pain, he took "handfuls of Tylenol." He could not wait for the insulin to take effect, so he started jogging in the middle of the night to lower his blood sugars. "It's two or three in the morning and I'm getting dressed for a jog. Afterward, I'd check my pulse and make sure that my heart rate was up so that my blood sugars would drop and the pain would go away." Sheer determination combined with an equally strong desire for pain relief enabled Max to do what for most people would be very difficult, if not impossible: to jog with severe pain.

Max's dreams and ambitions began to waver. "My schoolwork was absolutely nose-diving at this point. I'd been a reasonable student up to then. I had good study habits even in high school, and university wasn't that hard for me, though it was a lot more work. But now I was so exhausted that I had to drop all my classes." All that was important to Max began to change. His relationships changed: "I started snubbing friends so much that they stopped asking me out." His performance at work changed: "I tried to continue to go to work, but at this point I was in such severe pain in the abdomen that I was walking hunched over." His ability to care for himself changed: "I got so exhausted that I literally couldn't take care of myself—breakfast, dinner, whatever—I was so exhausted I wouldn't eat, plain and simple. If I had to get up and actually make food for myself, it just wouldn't get done." Max lived in that vortex of pain, sleeplessness, exhaustion and despair for six months.

Max told a very sobering story. Was it necessary for him to exist in that degree of pain for so long? Is it possible to control the pain that stems from a terminal illness?

Yes, it is possible. The medical literature has focused on people with cancer and AIDS, and doctors agree that for most people—eighty-five to ninety-five percent—pain can be controlled. So, why is it that so many people with these illnesses do experience pain? Some physicians lack adequate knowledge about pain medication (analgesics) and their side effects. Some are very cautious about prescribing the dose necessary to control the pain; some fear losing their license to practice medicine if they prescribe narcotics, and some keep to lower than necessary doses because of their concern about side effects. They might also fear that use of narcotics will lead to addiction.

Patients, on their part, can also be apprehensive about reporting pain or can feel that seeking out relief is a sign of weakness; often they have internalized the message to tough it out. Sometimes people avoid pain medication for religious or cultural reasons. They may fear addiction or the stigma of taking a narcotic, even if it is taken for legitimate reasons. Some lack access to adequate services.

Patients often speak of their pain. People with similar diagnoses may describe their pain quite differently from one another. If, as we listen, we use our own pain threshold as a reference point, we might dismiss or trivialize whatever the person is saying. This has become very apparent to me, not so much as a physician but as a parent. There are times when my children complain of pain that in my opinion simply doesn't seem to fit the injury they suffered. Thus I might try to toughen them up in the belief this is all "much ado about nothing," that they are seeking attention rather than responding appropriately. If I ignore them, brush them off, or if I do not appear to be interested in their long description of the pain they are experiencing, the children begin to learn that their pain will not be taken seriously. In fact, a child may feel ashamed of having pain or feel blamed for getting injured. (Pain is a natural response to injury; pain is not the fault of the person experiencing it.) Soon the child learns to live with the pain rather than to cry or express other feelings. Who benefits from that? The same question must be asked about patients. As a physician, it is important to set aside personal perceptions about the "appropriate" level of pain, as those perceptions may interfere with one's ability to fully appreciate the degree of pain that patients may experience.

Children who feel disregarded and helpless when a parent diminishes their experience of pain might exaggerate the next episode or fail to report it at all. Likewise, the physician who minimizes or doubts the patient's report jeopardizes that patient's trust and therefore the possibility of controlling the pain. And, like the hurt child, this patient might also feel trivialized and learn to live with the pain: "What's the use in telling the doctor about my pain, since he doesn't take me seriously, anyway?" they might ask. Or perhaps the patient, again like the hurt child, will exaggerate the pain to get attention. In either case, when the physician trivializes the pain, both the pain and mistrust are likely to increase.

All of us experience pain in our own way, but its ultimate effects are universal. When physical pain is present, it is virtually impossible to address spiritual or psychological concerns. When physical pain is present it becomes the focus of our existence. Anything and perhaps everything that might have been tranquil or peaceful ends with the presence of physical pain.

So if you are experiencing pain, it is important to express to your health-care providers as honestly and thoroughly as possible the nature of that pain and the ways it intrudes on other valued aspects of your life. All that is psychological or spiritual may be eclipsed by the pain you are experiencing.

Since the growth of hospice and palliative care programs, many people do not need to be admitted to the hospital for pain management. Teams working in the community are generally very effective in managing pain, symptoms (nausea, vomiting, constipation, etc.) and personal care (bathing, meal preparation, hygiene). In order to manage the pain, health-care providers must understand a variety of features about it. That is why they ask many questions about the pain.

Pain has a protective purpose. It is a warning sign of wounding or damage. It begins with a physical stimulus (damage to tissue or nerves), which is modified in the brain. It results in an awareness that something harmful or noxious is happening somewhere in the body. This results in an emotional response, a behavior that is associated with intense feelings of displeasure.

Because it is difficult to concentrate or remember details when you are having pain, it might be useful to jot down some notes about your experience before visiting your doctor.

What words would you use to describe the pain? What is the nature of the pain? Is it gnawing, aching, piercing, worst ever, tight, numbing, nagging, steady, like nothing I've ever experienced, similar to the pain I had when . . . If you are uncertain about what words describe your pain, choose a picture that comes to mind when you think about your pain— the pain feels (searing or hot) like a poker in a fire, the pain feels (sharp) like a knife going through my leg, I feel like there is an elephant (crushing pain) on my chest. You could also choose a color or a shape.

Where is the pain?

• Did the pain start in that location?

• Is it always there?

• Does it spread to other places in your body?

• Do you feel like every part of your body is uncomfortable, aching or painful?

Pain that feels like it's everywhere can mean that the source is difficult to identify. If the source is difficult to identify, or if your body really does hurt everywhere, describe the sensation as best you can—there are times when my whole body hurts"; "I get this aching throughout my body and there is nothing I can do to make it go away"; "every part of me hurts"; "I've never experienced anything like this before."

Is the pain present in several areas of the body at the same time?

When did the pain start?

• How long have you had the pain?

Pain is distinguished as being *acute*, meaning new or of recent onset, that is, present for a few hours or days; or *chronic*, meaning it has been present for many weeks, months or even years. People with chronic pain have often learned to live with pain and may not even describe the experience as painful. Rather they have "discomfort" or "depression"; they are "feeling blue" or they "used to feel different." If this sounds like you, it would help if you tried to remember when you last felt well, were free of discomfort and were able to do whatever you wanted without the ache or awareness of a particular muscle, joint or other body part.

Does the pain come and go (is it intermittent?) or is it always there (is it constant?)?

_____

_____

- Is it constant pain with episodes of more severity?

_____

_____

- Since the pain started, have you ever been pain-free? What have you tried—medication, treatments, exercise— to control the pain? Did anything work? How was the pain best controlled?

_____

_____

- Have you ever had pain like this before? What was the cause of the pain at that time? How was it controlled?

_____

_____

FACING DEATH, EMBRACING LIFE

While the pain was controlled, did you ever have pain for brief periods (so-called breakthrough pain)? What have you tried that didn't control the pain?

- What makes the pain worse (e.g., sitting, standing, walking, climbing stairs, lying down, eating)?

- What makes the pain better?

- Has it changed? If so, how?

- Does it change with activity? What are you not able to do because of the pain? What would you be doing if the pain were gone?

- Does it waken you from your sleep?

- Does it interfere with your work, daily activities or relationships with friends and family?

....

....

....

How severe is the pain?

- Looking at a scale (known as a "visual analogue scale") of 0–10, 0 being no pain and 10 being the worst pain you have ever had, how would you score the pain you have at present? Other scales might include descriptions like no pain, mild, moderate, severe, very severe, or worst possible pain; or perhaps none, annoying, uncomfortable, dreadful, horrible, or agonizing. Scales such as this are very important, as we can never really know the exact experience of pain that another person has. The scale becomes a reference point to the individual's experience of pain over time. A record of your pain could be valuable to those who are working with you to control the pain, a family or palliative care physician you might visit, or a home care nurse who might visit you in your home. In time, as you learn about how pain medication works, such a scale will also give you an understanding of how the dosage might need to be changed at certain times for you to keep being free of pain.

– 81 –

MORNING

0	1	2	3	4	5	6	7	8	9	10

No
Pain

Severe
Pain

AFTERNOON

0	1	2	3	4	5	6	7	8	9	10

No
Pain

Severe
Pain

EVENING

0	1	2	3	4	5	6	7	8	9	10

No
Pain

Severe
Pain

You could also have a 24-hour chart and write the number matching your pain on it at the particular time.

	SUN	MON	TUES	WEDS	THURS	FRI	SAT
AM							
1							
2							
3							
4							
5							
6							
7							
8							
9							
10							
11							
12							
PM							
1							
2							
3							
4							
5							
6							
7							
8							
9							
10							
11							
12							

Your doctor will likely ask you questions like these, but if she doesn't, think about these questions and compose answers that accurately express your experience; then offer them to the doctor. Write out your answers, or ask a friend or family member to do so. Your doctor should then do a physical exam, order some investigations if necessary, and prescribe pain-control medication. In many instances, especially in the home or hospice, a doctor will complete the assessment without ordering additional tests or investigations, as the trip to another facility can be problem-filled and even add to your pain and discomfort.

Perhaps there is some value in asking what there is to be learned from the pain we experience. What lesson is there to learn? How might I better understand myself and others through this experience? Those are difficult questions at the best of times, and perhaps even more difficult at the end of one's life.

Pain belongs to each and every one of us. It is part of our entry into the world, part of existing in the world and of departing from it. Pain has many faces. An athlete appreciates that pain is a likely part of training and competing; a pregnant woman can anticipate the pain that precedes the birth of her child with the realization that it will end with a baby in her arms; the patient welcomes the surgical removal of an inflamed appendix that has declared its presence with excruciating and nauseating pain; and the teenager with a broken arm knows that once the bone is set, healing will begin and the pain will eventually subside and disappear. Though some people experience a terminal illness without physical pain, it is, for many, part of living with such an illness. For some it is a constant, with no apparent pain-free end in sight. For others it is an intermittent reality, perhaps a fear and anxiety that pain is yet to come or will return. Pain is complex. It always has an emotional or psychological component.

This is what often happens with pain: one experiences a changed sense of self. Recall an old toothache or a migraine headache: it becomes virtually impossible to think of anything else but the sheer agony. Eventually, untreated pain will drain the joy out of life. Because pain becomes the focus of one's existence, it is important to ask, what would I be doing if I were pain-free, or what does this pain keep me from doing?

The following section is taken from my earlier book in the hope that it will serve as an easily accessible resource for you. Remember that most pain can be controlled! There are many and varied therapies for controlling pain. This section focuses on medication for pain control. Give the medication a chance to take effect and keep working with your health-care team to make the changes you need to get to a place of comfort.

There are many ways or routes by which to take pain medication: by mouth (oral) in the form of liquid, tablet, or sustained-release capsules; by rectum; across the skin by wearing a patch (transdermal); under the skin by a small needle (subcutaneous); through the veins (intravenous); with patient-controlled pumps; and small tubes (catheters) implanted in specific areas, such as the spine (epidural). Because of its cost-effectiveness and convenience, the oral route is preferred. It means people can stay at home, move around, and travel. But the other routes are important, as each patient has a unique disease experience and may benefit from different medications and routes. There is always some method that can be used to deliver pain medication.

The first medications used are not necessarily narcotics (also known as "opioids"). If the pain is mild, the doctor will likely recommend over-the-counter medications, with no prescription necessary: aspirin, acetaminophen, ibuprofen, and non-steroidal anti-inflammatory agents. It is always important to read the instructions and descriptions that come with the medication and to ask the pharmacist or doctor to identify the possible side effects. This becomes even more important when you are taking more than one medication (whether prescribed or over-the-counter) and when you have a history of liver disease, kidney disease, internal bleeding, allergies, stomach ulcers, substance abuse, or other problems that can affect the way the medication is processed (metabolized) in the body.

Apart from the side effects, there can be interactions specific to the combination of medications. Some of these can be beneficial, others harmful. Some people don't think of non-prescription medications as medicine and will forget to mention them to their doctor. Don't make this mistake! When you visit a doctor to manage pain, be sure to bring along a list of all the medications you are taking (both prescription and over-the-counter), noting the dosage of each. Always discuss the entire range of medication issues with your doctor to gain a clear understanding of the expected outcome and possible side effects. It is also valuable to understand how long before the medication takes effect; the same goes for side effects. Always be aware of possible interactions when taking more than one medication.

NAME OF DRUG	DOSAGE	FREQUENCY	PURPOSE	POSSIBLE SIDE EFFECTS
Morphine	10 mg	every 4 hours	Pain Control	Constipation, Drowsiness, Nausea
Ducosate	100mg	twice a day	Stool Softener	Diarrhea

Over-the-counter medications have ceiling effects, that is, a dose at which maximum benefit is achieved. If someone takes more than the maximum dose, that individual risks serious side effects. If the maximum dose is not effective, don't take more, and tell your doctor. In fact, inform your doctor whenever you approach the maximum dose. When non-prescription medications are no longer effective, the doctor will likely consider an opioid, such as codeine, morphine, hydromorphone (Dilaudid), oxycodone, fentanyl, or methadone. Morphine, an opioid, is effective and available, typically the first medication that a doctor will prescribe when an opioid is necessary.

It is generally more difficult to chase pain away than it is to stay on top of it. What does that mean? If you wait until the pain surfaces before taking medication, you will experience unnecessary discomfort; it is better to take medication on a regular basis to prevent the pain in the first place. When a doctor prescribes analgesics, the directions will be to take them on a regular basis, not on an as-needed basis. That means you will take medication every four, eight, or twelve hours (instructions are given when the medications are dispensed). Long-acting forms of medication are generally taken every eight or twelve hours. This means you don't have to interrupt your sleep to take it. For immediate-release medication, taken every four hours, you must wake from your sleep. This can be frustrating, but remember that it is easier to go back to sleep without pain; if pain wakens you, you will likely stay awake until the medication takes effect.

Even when pain is controlled, people can experience episodes of pain — breakthrough pain, also known as "incident pain," sometimes occurs because of physical activity; sometimes it is unpredictable; and sometimes it occurs just before the next regular dose of analgesic is due to be taken. Breakthrough pain requires a breakthrough dose of medication. Apart from the regular dose, then, it is important that your doctor also prescribes an as-needed dose to eliminate breakthrough pain. When someone is on regular medication, the breakthrough dose is usually taken an hour or two after the regular dose if the person experiences pain at that time.

A breakthrough dose may be necessary if you are taking regular pain medication, regardless of whether you are on immediate-release or sustained-release analgesics. Keep a record of how many breakthrough doses you take; mark the number on a calendar or in an appointment book and record the effects. Remember that some pain might not be related to the disease process. Maybe you had headaches before the disease, just as you might after the diagnosis. And though it's probably all right to take standard headache medication as you did before, be sure to check with your doctor.

Sometimes an activity (walking, bathing, sitting up for a visit) will cause pain. In those instances, pain might be prevented with a breakthrough dose taken twenty to thirty minutes before the activity takes place. (If your own breakthrough dose controls such pain, use the same dose the next time. If this makes you drowsy, consult with your nurse or physician about decreasing the dose the next time; if you still have pain, discuss increasing the dose.)

Understanding the concepts of pain management and working with your health-care providers will give you personal control and a better sense of well-being. Try to find a professional who will work with you. Contact a local hospice or palliative care association, ask family members and friends, or consult health services in your area. The appropriate dose of opioid is the amount that relieves the pain, provided side effects are minimal or at least tolerable. As the dose increases, side effects become more likely. However, each person is unique and will experience side effects differently. If the side effects are intolerable, ask your doctor to treat them. To do so, you might need to introduce another medication (in addition or in substitution). That way the dose of opioid can be increased if necessary.

Common side effects from opioids are constipation, nausea, vomiting and drowsiness. Some people also experience confusion and, on high doses, muscle twitching (myoclonus). Opioids generally act on the gastrointestinal tract (movement is slowed and secretions are diminished). That combined with decreased physical activity, less fluid intake, and diet contribute to constipation. A rule of thumb: at a minimum, people need a bowel movement every three days. Constipation can be difficult to resolve—stool softeners or laxatives may be needed. It helps to drink fluids, especially fruit juices; also, you can eat fruit, bran, and any other foods that have been beneficial in the past. As opioid doses are increased, the doses of softeners and laxatives are usually increased as well. For most people, constipation is uncomfortable. As with pain, it is better to prevent constipation beforehand than to treat it after the fact. For this reason, we routinely prescribe constipation medication at the same time that an opioid is prescribed.

When people first start on an opioid, they may experience nausea and vomiting. Opioid-associated nausea occurs for several reasons: physiological response, the taste of the drug, fears and concerns about opioids, or anxiety that the opioid is a sure sign that the disease is progressing. Nausea and vomiting can generally be treated with an anti-emetic medication, usually taken before the opioid. As with constipation, have a strategy for dealing with nausea and vomiting. If your doctor doesn't prescribe an anti-emetic or laxative when first prescribing opioids, raise the subject yourself. "I've heard that people who take medications for pain often get constipated and some people feel nauseated when they take them. What might I do if that happens to me?"

Having instructions about over-the-counter medications or having a prescription in hand for constipation and nausea could serve you well. This may actually reduce your anxiety. For most people the nausea and vomiting will decrease or clear up entirely in a week or two, and then the medication for those symptoms can be reduced or eliminated.

Many people experience drowsiness when they first take an opioid. Essentially this happens for two reasons. First, the drug affects the central nervous system; and second, people who have lived with pain are usually exhausted from that experience. When they get to be pain-free, they relax and with the relief comes the overwhelming need to sleep. The drowsiness usually clears up in a day or two, but it can take longer. If drowsiness persists for more than seventy-two hours, check with your doctor. He may need to decrease the dose or switch to an alternate medication. Your doctor should tell you what to expect, and you in turn should inform friends and family about such things as side effects, treatment, benefits of the medication, the timeframe and changing medication. Without this information, they may be surprised and concerned that you actually seem sicker after taking an opioid. They will also benefit from a reminder that pain can occur at any time during a terminal illness, regardless of your outward appearance, and that your drowsiness will likely clear in a few days.

In some instances, people who take opioids become confused or experience delirium. Some may have hallucinations. Such symptoms can also be caused by the spread of the cancer to the brain, compromised function of the liver, kidneys or lungs, and changes in metabolism that occur as a result of the disease. If it is determined that confusion or delirium is a result of the opioid, the dose can be reduced or an alternate opioid can be tried. Symptoms caused by one opioid might not occur with another. The older you are, the more likely you are to experience confusion and delirium. Therefore, dosages might be increased more gradually. However, if the pain is severe or has been present for a long time, you might welcome the relief despite the side effects. For most people, side effects can be managed, leading to better overall quality of life.

Very high doses of opioids can lead to muscle-twitching (myoclonus), not unlike the muscle twitching that occurs just prior to falling asleep. For some, the twitching interferes with their activities, so it may be of value for your doctor to add a muscle relaxant. If the twitching is severe and cannot be controlled with a muscle relaxant, discuss this with your doctor, who may consider switching to an alternative opioid. Often the twitching is more problematic for friends and family sitting at the bedside than it is for the person experiencing the twitching.

One of the greatest concerns people have with opioids is addiction. Some people are initially hesitant and refuse them simply on that basis. If you are taking an opioid as prescribed, you will rarely become an addict. Addiction is a psychological disorder. It is based on the craving for and the compulsive use of a substance that has mind-altering or psychic effects. Often, the addict seeks an altered state of consciousness with the hope of escaping into euphoria.

If you have ever experienced pain in your lifetime, you know that people with pain seek to be pain-free. The opioid is intended to achieve that outcome. As long as pain is present, the effects of the opioid will work and an altered euphoric state will not occur. The point is not to alter your state of consciousness but to manage your pain. Thus the likelihood of addiction is minimized.

Tolerance and physical dependence can be mistaken for addiction. "Tolerance" means that the dose of pain medication will need to be increased over time in order to keep the effects of analgesia. This is actually a useful feature of opioids, in that tolerance results in clearing the side effects. "Physical dependence" occurs to all people who take opioids. It means only that the body gets used to having the medication present and that the medication must never be stopped suddenly. If opioids are stopped suddenly, the person is more likely to experience symptoms of withdrawal—nausea, diarrhea, muscle aches and pains, and general discomfort. The person is not left with a craving for euphoria or the need to have the medication. For recovering addicts, their addiction must be taken into account when reducing opioids. If you are a recovering addict, make sure your physician understands your history in this regard.

Apart from opioids, many other medications are used to manage and control pain. As an example, the pain experienced when a nerve has been affected by the disease process is known as "neuropathic pain." It is often described as burning or searing. Neuropathic pain is effectively treated with medications usually used for depression (antidepressants) and seizures (anticonvulsants); steroids are also helpful.

Doctors practice medicine with the intent of curing disease, eliminating pain and suffering, and working toward an optimal quality of life for the patient. Every medication and treatment, although intended to do good, can also have a harmful side effect. It is difficult to anticipate every side effect, but it is helpful to have a general sense of what to expect. That's why it is important to ask your doctor about side effects and to inform her if you have experienced side effects from other medications.

Once their physical pain is controlled, people can shift their focus to other concerns and issues in their lives, whether emotional, mental or spiritual.

In summary, pain is part of living with a terminal illness. For some, pain is a constant reality, however well controlled. For others it occurs occasionally. And for some it is only the fear or dread of what might happen. In any case, pain cannot be ignored. If pain is present, it can usually be alleviated. Medication is one component of controlling or managing pain. Other components might include acupuncture, Transcutaneous Electrical Nerve Stimulation (TENS), visualization exercises, meditation, physiotherapy and music therapy.

In those few instances when pain is not controlled, it must be addressed. All possible interventions must be considered as a means to diminish the pain. In the rare cases where even that is not possible, there are ways to increase pain medications and add sedatives so that people are not conscious in their pain experience. These cases are the most difficult for me personally. The occurrence of uncontrollable pain is one of the uncomfortable realities that led me to explore the spiritual and psychological issues of living with terminal illness. It is difficult to sit in the presence of a person with uncontrolled pain. At times the anguish is unbearable. At that point, asking for help from any and all sources is imperative. No one with pain ought to be left to experience it alone.

Remember that pain is always a combination of physical and psychological features, and for some it has a spiritual component as well. Pain must be assessed from the perspective of wholeness, and that includes our physical, psychological and spiritual well-being. Only then can the pain be eliminated and the suffering reduced such that one can achieve an optimal quality of life.

FOUR

Being Touched, Being in Touch

In touching one another we make a connection. One of the strongest messages I received from people living with a terminal illness was that connection was of great importance: connection to themselves in knowing themselves, connection to others in intimate relationships, and a sense of connection to something greater than themselves, that is, a spiritual entity. Through touch—both touching and being touched—healing begins. Thereby, suffering is reduced; pain is altered. One person touching another affects both people. For many who live with a terminal illness, social roles have been lost and relationships irrevocably altered. For them, perhaps even more so than at other times of life, touch plays an important role in reconnecting with others and in creating new relationships. Being in touch/ touching might be regarded as a verbal and a physical act. In some instances the words we speak might be as appropriate and effective as the touch of a hand!

Remember a time when the touch of another human being was essential to your sense of well-being. Who was the person? What were the circumstances? Was it spontaneous or by request?

What is the significance of human contact, of touch, to you?

In an interview with Bill Moyers in 1993, Rachel Remen, a doctor who has been working for more than twenty years with people who have terminal illnesses and the author of *Kitchen Table Wisdom* and *My Grandfather's Blessings*, begins to answer that question. She speaks of touching as a way of healing. She acknowledges that we don't touch each other a lot and, when we do, that it's often misunderstood or sexualized. As Bill Moyers writes, "Touch is deeply reassuring and nurturing. It's the first way a mother and child connect with each other . . . What a mother is saying to her child with that touch is 'Live . . . your life matters to me.'"

Marjorie, who was in her early seventies, attended support groups at a cancer center. She also attended week-long retreats for persons with life-threatening illnesses. She observed that "touch is a necessity of life. We need to be touched. When you attend one of the group meetings, prepare yourself, because there's a lot of touching going on there, and I think it's magical. I really do feel that if it isn't physically healing, it is certainly emotionally and psychologically healing." This was in direct contrast to her experience when she was admitted to the hospital for a medical procedure. "There was nobody to be with me, to hold my hand and tell jokes or anything. It was the most horrifying experience."

Marjorie felt that, through the touch of another person, a sense of togetherness was created and healing could occur. During her medical procedures in the hospital, her friend's voice also contributed to a pain-free experience, even though she couldn't remember what her friend had been speaking about; the content of what her friend said was not important. She also recommended that doctors touch patients in a reassuring way as part of providing care for the patient.

We experience touch through our skin, the largest sensory organ of the human body. The human embryo develops from three cell layers: the endoderm, the mesoderm, and the ectoderm, the latter being the outer layer. This layer gives rise to the nervous system and to the general surface covering the body—hair, nails, teeth, skin—and to the sense organs of smell, taste, hearing, vision and touch. One of the primary functions of the central nervous system is to keep the organism informed about what is going on outside the organism. The nerve endings in the skin send signals or messages via the spinal cord to the brain. The brain analyzes the information, interpreting the effect of the touch. The brain then informs the rest of the body about the response it will have to the touch. Interestingly, the skin also informs the world outside the organism about what is going on within the organism. As a physician, features such as the color, temperature, texture, moistness and dryness, thickness and elasticity of the skin give me information about what is going on under the skin and within the body.

The functions of the skin include temperature control, protection, metabolic functions and sensation. Touch is essential not only for the newborns but also for children, adolescents and adults. In the nineteenth century, the death rate for babies abandoned to institutions was very high. After 1915, doctors made rules requiring that babies be picked up and carried around several times a day. Handling, carrying, caressing, caregiving and cuddling were fundamental to the infant's survival.

Self-esteem is partly based on bodily relationship and connectedness, beginning in infancy and continuing through childhood and adolescence. Montagu's book *Touching* includes a report by Dr. Jimmie Holland, who early in her career worked with leukemia patients at the University of Buffalo School of Medicine. In order to prevent all skin contact between patients and others, the patients were isolated in germ-free rooms as part of their treatment. They could look out of the rooms and could be seen from without. They used verbal communication facilities to interact with people outside their rooms. Seventy-five percent of the patients "experienced an acute sense of isolation, chiefly related to the inability to touch or be touched directly. The loss of human physical contact generated feelings of loneliness, frustration, a sense of coldness, and a lack of emotional warmth." Physical contact—that is, touch—is an essential ingredient to a sense of emotional connectedness.

Terminally ill people also need to be touched. For some people, emotional connection begins with physical touch.

Dr. Lewis Thomas, former president of Memorial Sloan-Kettering Cancer Center in New York City, wrote in the early 1980s that touching is a real professional secret, an essential skill and "the most effective act of doctors."

Some people don't like being handled by others, but that seems to be less so for people who are sick. They need to be touched, and part of the dismay in being very sick is the lack of close human contact. Ordinary people, close friends, even family members, tend to stay away from the very sick, touching them as infrequently as possible for fear of interfering or catching the illness or just for fear of bad luck. The doctor's oldest skill was to place his hands on the patient.

Touch is the strongest nonverbal message that one person can give to another. But how does touch occur when it's not already a part of an existing relationship, when it hasn't happened prior to knowing that someone has a terminal illness? One way that it begins is by asking to be touched or for permission to touch, as in: "Can I hold your hand as we speak?" "Do you mind if I put my arm around you?" "May I hold you?"

Being touched or held can be something you want and at the same time it may be something you fear or feel awkward about. This might arise from your personality or it may be due to the setting, such as a hospital. If you long for touch (or more of it), I encourage you to speak to someone you trust, someone likely to understand. It may mean that you ask someone you care about to hold your hand the next time you are together or it might mean that someone holds you as you sit or lie next to one another. It might also mean a hug when greeting or parting company. For some people this is natural, for others uncomfortable. Discomfort can stem from the absence of touch in your life or from painful experiences of touch in your past, but it is never too late to start anew. Touch is essential to one's sense of well-being. "Nurturing," "touch," and "connection" are synonymous.

Start simply: sit across the table and hold hands as you speak. This may seem foreign, and you may only feel comfortable with one or two people you know. If you try this, tell the other person how you feel: "I feel close to you and would like to hold your hand or sit next to you, but I want to respect you and not impose myself upon you. I would like to hold your hand as we speak." Next, do the same thing, but without the table; sit facing each other, knees touching, holding hands, and begin a conversation. Eventually you may feel comfortable without even speaking. Perhaps you can relate a story from your past describing how touch was important to your sense of well-being. In that connection, you may both feel reassured.

Family members have often said to me, "No one told me to hold or touch my mother" (or father, brother, sister, friend). "No one told me it was all right to lie beside the person, holding them. It's what I really wanted to do, but it felt awkward, so I didn't do it. But after the person died I was very sorry and regretted not having followed my own instinct." It's important to let others know about your wishes now. Be mindful that touch is of value both to the person touching and to the person being touched.

People who are dying often feel out of touch physically and emotionally. They feel that no one else knows or understands their experience. They feel isolated. They crave physical contact, not merely as a means of physical comfort or pain relief, but more significantly as a way to counteract the feeling of being untouchable and separate. I have learned that the primary importance of touch is as an antidote to isolation and despair. "Being in touch" means that I know that another person knows my experience of living with a terminal illness. Being touched and being in touch are experiences of the present, experiences of now.

There is great value of being physically touched by another person and of being emotionally in touch, that is, emotionally connected with people who care for you and who are going to be involved in your care, people who work to know and understand you as a person living with a terminal illness.

Some people who know they have a terminal illness feel out of touch—out of touch with who they were before, out of touch with the people they care about and who care about them, out of touch with normal life, out of touch with their God. It is a sense of estrangement from the familiar, the beginning of a process of increasing isolation. The physical touch of another person counteracts that sense of aloneness, that sense of being out of touch and of being untouchable. Physical contact—touch—eliminates the space between two people.

What is the loneliness of knowing you have a terminal illness? Does it pertain to your sense of leaving people behind, or does it perhaps pertain to your sense that, while there are others around you, the journey before you is one that only you can travel?

If you have a terminal illness and are reading this book, you may know the answer to that question. For you it may include feelings of being untouchable or an awareness that those you love are afraid that if they touch you they might get sick as well. It may also include tears of sadness, grief, and nostalgia for the past, for the way that life was and will never be again. You have likely experienced an intermittent panic and perhaps a sense of guilt because of the finite amount of time you have left to accomplish what seems like an infinite number of tasks. And there is the despair and isolation of realizing that you must say goodbye not to just one person but to all the family members and friends who have been significant over the course of your lifetime. Fear associated with being alone, with the loss of intimacy, with a sense of abandonment, may keep you awake at night. Being touched and being in touch can serve to counteract that.

The fear of abandonment or of being misunderstood stems in part from the emotions that emerge whenever the topic of death is introduced into a conversation. The topic of death calls forth some very deep feelings that define, more accurately than words, who we are. These feelings may not have been known to us or expressed to others before the diagnosis was made.

What do I feel when the topic of death is part of a conversation? Do I dare to experience those feelings now?

....

....

....

....

....

How might I risk sharing those feelings with another person?

....

....

....

....

If I let other people know how I feel, how are they likely to respond? Might I be rejected by them for telling them how I feel?

....

....

....

....

How do I move from this place of aloneness to a place of intimacy or closeness?

....

....

....

....

Where do I begin?

....

....

....

....

Ultimately, no one can protect us from the reality of death, our own death. On an existential level, we are indeed alone. Only

FACING DEATH, EMBRACING LIFE

in the womb are all our needs met by another. We are born with a longing to recover that same sense of connection, first with our parents, and then perhaps in relationship to others.

In part, it is because friends and family members avoid the topic of death that people who have a terminal illness feel alone and out of touch. Health-care providers also avoid the topic of death.

For those who want to begin to understand the experience of loneliness, imagine what it would be like to give up the things you enjoy doing the most—playing a sport, going for a walk with a close friend, reading books, holding your child, carrying your grandchild, listening to music. Imagine not being able to complete any of the tasks you are now working on or would like to work on in the next three to six months. Imagine visiting each one of your friends and family members who are important to you, holding conversations (as per the above exercise) as if you would never see them again. Imagine lying awake at night staring into the darkness with a new and painful sense of awareness that you are not immortal, that neither love nor science can stop the disease process within you. Imagine feeling the apprehension other people have about being in your presence or touching you. Imagine feeling alone and lonely. I invite you to take some time to write about your thoughts and imaginings.

– 104 –

The sense of aloneness that people who have a terminal illness experience, and the desire they have to speak about dying, became apparent through a study done in the early 1980s by Dr. David Spiegel of Stanford Medical School in California. He conducted a study with a group of women who had breast cancer. From his extensive clinical work, Dr. Spiegel informed us that people with cancer could experience a feeling of isolation, among other feelings, such as grief and pain. Some family members and friends withdraw from people with cancer because they are afraid that it may be contagious, that they can catch the cancer. They may feel awkward and inept in dealing with a situation that conjures up difficult emotions or challenging physical realities. They may also feel a high level of anxiety about the impending death of someone close to them.

People with AIDS have the same experience. In fact, the isolation experienced by people who have AIDS is often more extreme, because of the higher level of anxiety the disease creates in others. (Imagine what it feels like when you sense that those you love and who love you avoid hugging or holding you, giving you a kiss, shaking your hand, caressing or massaging your body.) Some family members stand at the foot of the bed or sit in a chair at a considerable distance. Others prefer to stay outside the room entirely. In 1989, Amanda Heggs, a woman with AIDS, was quoted in the London *Guardian:* "Sometimes I have a terrible feeling that I am dying not from the virus, but from being untouchable."

Dr. Spiegel invited women with metastatic breast cancer (spread beyond the primary site) to participate in a psychological support group that would meet weekly for ninety minutes. Each group consisted of seven to ten women and had two leaders, one a psychiatrist or social worker, the other a counselor who had breast cancer in remission at the time. The purpose of the support group was to focus on discussions of death and dying, related family problems, difficulties in obtaining treatment, issues of communication with physicians, and living as fully as possible with the knowledge that they had a terminal illness. They worked together to explore their relationships with family members, to admit to and discuss their fears, to learn from each other about life lessons encountered as a result of having a terminal illness, and to face their own deaths. They shared their grief as members of the group grew sicker or died. Knowing they had a terminal illness, and having leaders who were helpful and comfortable in confronting death and dying, enabled the group members to keep on task.

Dr. Spiegel and his colleagues worked to create an

atmosphere in which the women could talk about the difficult topics, the issues and feelings that seemed to be unspeakable in their homes and among friends. They watched carefully for signs of emotion, for someone who looked as though they might start crying, for someone who looked worried and was unable to speak about the cause. It was these women who were encouraged to speak, these issues that the leaders focused on—the very issues that the participants had not been able to discuss with anyone else. In working together to face common problems these women became "less anxious, confused, fatigued and fearful."

Talking about the experience of having a terminal illness changes the anxiety and fear; it diminishes the loneliness and isolation. Many of the people who participated in my study would say, "I've never spoken about this to anyone." Another response was, "I feel better after talking to you today." Once people knew they had a terminal illness, they wanted to talk about it—to be in touch, emotionally and physically, with at least one other person. In some peculiar way, it seemed that the loneliness served a purpose for some people. These people began to identify what was really important to them. They started a process of being in touch with their own inner selves.

Here is another timeline or life-line exercise. Draw the time-line. Place an X one centimeter to the left of the word Death, and then add a dotted line *beyond* the word Death. The dotted line represents the emotional legacy you will leave others after you have died.

Birth————————————————————*X—Death* - - - - -

Again, write your name below the X. What are you feeling as you write your name?

_____
_____
_____
_____

Name five people you love.

1. _____
2. _____
3. _____
4. _____
5. _____

You might write the names of these people above the X. What do you feel as you write each person's name? What are your thoughts about the limited time that remains?

_____
_____
_____

What would you like to say to this person?

_____
_____
_____

What would you like to hear from this person?

_____
_____

What would you like to do together during the time remaining in your life?

What do you most value about this individual?

What are your favorite memories that include this person?

What are some of the awkward, painful or difficult times and experiences you have shared? What did you gain or lose from those experiences together?

How has your life been richer because this person is part of your life?

_____

_____

_____

_____

How has the other person's life been richer because you are part of their life? What has your relationship given to them that will be present in them, even after you die? (I.e., What is the legacy you leave that will continue in them after you die?)

_____

_____

_____

_____

The Family Meeting

There are many decisions to make once someone has been told that they have a terminal illness. Every person in this situation would benefit from having a friend or family member who will act as an advocate. Often people feel overwhelmed and alone in making necessary decisions, wondering how to involve those they care about, at times fearful of asking for help from others. These decisions and choices pertain to more than just the disease and the treatment that might reverse, stop or slow down the process; they also pertain to the life you want to lead in the amount of time and with the energy remaining. In fact, the unfinished business, your sense of self, and your relationship with others may be just as important, or even more so, than focusing all your attention on the disease. It is crucial to remember that the choices belong to you, the person with the illness. And living is a dynamic process, so you can always make new decisions and can change your mind about past ones.

Five Steps toward a Community of Support

If you have a life-threatening or terminal illness, or if you are getting on in years and would like to have a meeting with significant people to discuss your future, the five-step process outlined below can benefit you. I have used it with many families in the hospital, with friends and in my own family.

In many instances, dying requires a community of support. It could be years, months, weeks or days before you die. Depending on the prognosis, you might meet regularly— every month or two or with longer intervals between meetings. You might feel awkward or uncomfortable initially, perhaps because you do not want to inconvenience people. However, my experience is that people are generally relieved when someone invites them into a meaningful conversation. It usually benefits all who participate, often strengthening friendships and family relationships. The process keeps people connected and informed about what is happening, about your wishes, and about how they can be a part of your care plan.

Family members might not be accustomed to speaking openly and honestly about wishes for health care and dying, which means others will be left to guess. So when you invite people over, make certain they understand the purpose: to have an open discussion about living with dying, about making decisions that will affect how you lead the remainder of your life. The end of life usually involves friends and family members. Your relationships with people before you die will affect how they grieve after you die. Unfinished business may complicate the grieving process, for you before you die and for others after you die. I encourage you to participate in a process like this. You could also tape (audio or video) a message for your family and friends. If this is something you do not want to do or cannot do, it would still be of value to think about the discussion topics that follow and write down what you would like to have happen in a variety of circumstances.

The process I present here is based on work that was taught and written about by three American ethicists: Albert Jonsen, Mark Siegler and William Winslade. These three developed a decision-making process to help ethics committees in hospitals resolve ethical dilemmas. Their work has been adapted at St. Paul's Hospital in Vancouver to include families and professionals in these and other decisions. Initially it was used to resolve ethical dilemmas. It has also been useful in making complex decisions at the end of life. We invite patients and those who are important to them to join the health-care team in developing a plan for the patient.

a. Organizing the Meeting

To conduct a decision-making meeting, invite the people who are important to you—close family members and friends. Make a list of all the people you would like to invite to your home for the meeting. This is not a family gathering, nor a party. It is a meeting with a purpose. People who are invited are generally those who have been supportive to you through your lifetime, especially in the most recent years.

1. ....
2. ....
3. ....
4. ....
5. ....
6. ....
7. ....
8. ....
9. ....
10. ....
11. ....
12. ....
13. ....
14. ....
15. ....

You might ask a close friend or family member to phone everyone, explaining the purpose of the meeting. Guests could also be asked to bring some food so the group could share a meal together after the meeting. Usually all those who are invited make a serious effort to attend and are both pleased and honored to do so.

Invite professionals (e.g., physician, home care nurse, minister, rabbi, or priest) who know you and are involved in providing care for you. (The meeting will have value even if they can't attend.)

The meeting can be organized by you, a family member, or a friend. Set the time, date and place. The process usually takes two to three hours. Because facilitating a meeting requires a lot of energy, it is wise to ask someone in advance to act as facilitator. (If you know of someone with experience and skills in facilitation, invite that person to act on your behalf.) That way your energy can be spent on the decisions that need to be made, rather than on keeping a group of people focused and on topic. Everyone involved must understand that the purpose of the meeting is to develop a health-care plan for you.

It is important for the facilitator to keep the discussion moving in a respectful manner and to make certain that everyone present is given the opportunity to express opinions and raise concerns. The goal is to develop a comprehensive plan, with those present making a commitment to the plan and therefore making a commitment to you. It might also be wise to invite someone who is attending the meeting to be the recorder. Consider asking someone who can record the information on the flip chart in a legible fashion to be the recorder.

Once all the participants have gathered, make sure they are comfortable and all within easy speaking range of each other. Sitting in a circle helps. Introduce the facilitator, explain that you invited this person, and, if you like, why you chose that person. Next, ask participants to introduce themselves and describe their relationship to you.

This is a very intense process. If at any time you feel too tired to proceed, ask to take a break or that the meeting end for now, and arrange to meet at another time. If you are too tired to concentrate, you will have trouble knowing what you really want.

The facilitator begins by describing the process and the purpose of the meeting, and identifying any decisions that need to be made. It is helpful for the facilitator to set a few guidelines for the conversation:

- Be sure participants know that they will be invited to contribute and will have an opportunity to speak or ask questions. Be sure they understand that you welcome and value their opinions.

- Explain that it is important to speak respectfully.

- Remind participants to be aware that communication is both verbal and nonverbal; people are invited to speak clearly and simply so that all those in attendance can understand; gestures such as rolled eyes, raised eyebrows, grunts of disapproval and the like are not welcome.

- Ask everyone to make a commitment to stay until the end of the meeting. If someone is called away for an emergency, ask if the person has anything to add before they leave.

- If at all possible, pagers and cell phones should be turned off; you want people's undivided attention.

Record everything discussed on a large flip chart so that everyone can see the information. It is also important to keep a "to do" list; add to it throughout the process.

If it is difficult to gather people in one place, another possibility is to conduct the meeting over the Internet via a chat room or by e-mail. Some people follow up the first meeting with an e-mail communication.

Imagine that the meeting is taking place in your living room or family room: you are surrounded by family members and friends who care about you, who are willing to do some work on your behalf, and who want to keep in touch through the course of your illness, your remaining lifetime. You cannot predict what all your needs will be or the exact course your illness will take. No one can do that. Unfortunately, for some the health-care system will not be user-friendly. In fact, it can show indifference and even antagonism, despite your circumstances. Therefore, you might need a strong advocate to speak and intervene on your behalf. I strongly encourage you to invite one or two people to act as your advocates as necessary throughout the course of your illness. The people around you are the people who will understand you, who will know what you want and how you prefer to live. Some of them will make a commitment to work with you in meeting needs, accomplishing goals and speaking for you. Although this may be a difficult meeting, it is a very important one, for you as well as for all those people who love you.

Once the stage is set and introductions have taken place, ask if there are any questions people might have.

b. Medical Information

The recorder puts this title on the flip chart for this part of the discussion. You should speak first, if possible. Inform the group about your health. Perhaps a close friend or family member has accompanied you to doctor's appointments; ask him or her to speak on your behalf or add to your comments. Go over the facts of your medical history and explain what has happened to you to require a meeting like this.

Report on all the symptoms, the tests and the results.

What is the diagnosis (the name of the disease) and the prognosis (the future course of the disease)?

....

....

....

What treatments have you had to date? If you're talking about cancer, options would include surgery, chemotherapy and radiation therapy. Inform the group about any alternative therapies you have tried.

....

....

....

....

....

If your health-care providers are present, they would likely be willing to assist you in providing and explaining the information about your medical condition and history to the group. Invite them to do so.

The facilitator asks the questions. The recorder jots notes on the flip chart so everyone can see and understand the topic of discussion. Often, speaking about these issues helps to clarify what is important to you.

Which therapies are you considering? What are the risks? What will your life be like if you have the therapy you are considering? What will it be like if you don't?

If surgery is an option, how long will the recovery period be? Do you want to spend that amount of time recovering, given the best estimate of your life expectancy at this point? How might your daily life improve if the surgery results in the most desirable outcome?

If chemotherapy or radiation therapy is an option, or if there is some medication that might have an effect on the illness, what is the timeframe in which the treatment would take effect?

• What is the earliest point at which you might benefit?

- How long would you have to be on the medication before you would know whether it was working?

  ....

  ....

- What are the side effects of treatment? How are they managed? How long do they usually last?

  ....

  ....

  ....

- How soon would treatments have to begin in order to have some effect on the disease process? Is the disease progressing so quickly that waiting to start the treatment might mean that it would not have any benefit?

  ....

  ....

  ....

Has your doctor spoken to you about your life expectancy? If so, be brave enough to include the information you have been given in that regard.

  ....

  ....

  ....

Is there any aspect of your illness that is reversible?

  ....

  ....

  ....

If you are in pain, how is it being managed? What are other options? (See Chapter 3.)

And what about other symptoms, such as shortness of breath (dyspnea), constipation, nausea, vomiting, fatigue or insomnia? What might you expect as the disease progresses? How are these symptoms being treated right now? Are there other possibilities? Every alternative you consider important should be included: physiotherapy, acupuncture, therapeutic touch, meditation, homeopathy and so on.

What has been your experience with the health-care system? Do you usually have to wait a long time to see your physician, to have tests conducted, to receive results? Do you sometimes get information by phone or do you have to visit your doctor for every question?

- If you are frustrated with the care you have been receiving, or with a lack of information, what changes need to be made? How might that happen?

- Do you need someone to act as an advocate? Are you getting the information you need, and is it presented in a way that is easily understood? Do you believe that you understand all your options? How much time and energy are you spending to obtain the information you want and need with regard to your health and treatment options?

How well can you live a normal life? What would that look like? What do you miss most about the life you were living before you got sick?

- Are you self-sufficient? Do you need help with grocery shopping, preparing meals or personal hygiene—bathing or washing your hair, getting dressed? Can you go out as often as you'd like to? Does it take too much energy? Do you need someone to go with you? Have you noticed any changes in this regard over the past months, weeks or days? If not now, do you think you will need assistance in the near or distant future if things progress at the current rate? Who would be able to assist you, should you require some help? Would an assessment by an occupational therapist regarding your daily activities be of value? Who could help you arrange that?

What features of this experience contribute to your suffering? Is it the changes, the sense of loss, becoming dependent on others, fears about the future? What is affecting or changing your sense of self and/or your relationships with the people who are important to you?

You may not have all the answers to these questions. You may have additional questions. But if these questions have sparked a desire for more information from your doctor, who may not be present, invite someone along to your next visit with your doctor. Make a list of the questions you would like to ask. Make sure the facilitator invites people to contribute or ask questions at specific points, especially if some people are shy about asking questions. It is important to gather as much information as is available, as this will contribute to establishing a plan.

c. Your Preferences

Add this heading to the flip chart. The first part of the process focused on presenting the medical information. In the second part, you can review the choices you need to make and the actions you need to take with regard to the options discussed.

Do you want to go ahead with the treatment plan your doctor has outlined? Would you like a second opinion?

Will the treatment really make a difference? What are your goals (cure, palliation, prolong your life) with regard to the treatment?

How will you know that the disease has progressed? What are the features of the natural history of the disease?

....

....

....

Are there treatment options that are known to have a very low success rate that you would like to learn more about or that you would like to consider seriously? What would be necessary to persuade you to have a certain treatment or to dismiss it as an option? Do you need to try all treatments regardless of their success, simply because you are someone who doesn't quit? How might that affect those who care about you with regard to your physical, emotional and spiritual energy?

....

....

....

....

....

Most people begin with the wish for a cure, even when they know that the disease is incurable. Working toward a cure can include one more effort with a particular therapy. Some people place a lot of hope in that magic cure, the one with a five-percent chance of reversing the disease process. In some instances family members or friends have a strong wish for their loved one to pursue every treatment they hear about. How will you have discussions about these treatments? How will you decide about pursuing them or not pursuing them?

....

....

....

....

....

....

....

Are you focused on that magical cure because that's what you want or because that's what your partner/spouse/children want you to do? Is your focus on the magic cure distracting you from other important issues that require your time and attention right now?

....

....

....

....

....

It is of value to dream out loud about what you would like to do in the time you have left. Although this can be a rewarding process, it is usually an emotionally painful process as well. Your preferences in this regard will reflect who you are as an individual (activities you would like to enjoy one more time; something new you have not tried before), your relationships with others (special events such as birthdays, graduations and weddings; conversations that you need to have; time with favorite people), and your sense of spirituality (meaning, forgiveness, meditation, self-reflection, worship). And while you are expressing your dreams and desires, you may also experience a sense of grief because you recognize some real and some potential losses.

What are some of your other goals? Are there things you really want to do or see? Some people want to travel to a particular place because of certain memories. Some want to travel to visit family members or friends. Sometimes there are conversations people want to have while they have enough energy to do so. You might want to divide these goals into personal goals, goals that relate to family and friends and goals that pertain to the spiritual domain.

Personal goals:

....

....

....

....

....

....

Goals pertaining to important relationships (family and friends):

....

....

....

....

....

....

Goals pertaining to your spiritual life:

....

....

....

....

....

....

....

How might your health-care team help you achieve these goals? If they are not present at the meeting, tell everyone about your entire health-care team—all those who provide physical, spiritual and psychological care and support—family members, friends, volunteers and professionals. In a way, you are introducing them to the people they will likely meet through the course of your illness.

....

....

....

....

....

....

Have you considered palliative or hospice care? Do you want those services, and are they available in your community? How might you get information about the hospice or palliative care program in your community? Is there anyone (doctor, nurse, occupational therapist, physiotherapist, pastoral care, volunteer) who does home visits from that organization?

....

....

....

....

....

....

What about advance directives (documents outlining or expressing your wishes for health-care decisions if you are incapacitated)? The intent of these directives is to give you control over decisions in the future, should you become unable to communicate your wishes regarding your health care.

....

....

....

....

....

....

Your illness experience may have a reversible and an irreversible component to it. For instance, someone with a brain tumor might experience an episode of pneumonia. Both of those disease processes might cause the person's death. Pneumonia can usually be treated with antibiotics. For many people with advanced cancer, the pneumonia would be the cause of death if left untreated.

With regard to the irreversible component of a terminal illness (eg. cancer), what type of care would you like with regard to use of:

treatment to prolong your life?

_____

_____

_____

_____

treatment to keep you comfortable (palliative care)?

_____

_____

_____

_____

blood transfusions?

_____

_____

food (feeding tubes, IV, supplements)?

_____

_____

_____

cardiopulmonary resuscitation (CPR)?

_____

_____

_____

Where would you like to receive care?

admission/transfer to hospital?

_____

_____

_____

_____

admission/transfer to ICU?

_____

_____

_____

_____

admission/transfer to a hospice?

_____

_____

_____

_____

admission to a palliative care unit?

_____

_____

_____

_____

With regard to the reversible component (eg. pneumonia) of a terminal illness, what type of care would you like with regard to use of:

antibiotics (oral, IV)?

treatment to prolong your life?

treatment to keep you comfortable (palliative care)?

blood transfusions?

food (feeding tubes, IV, supplements)?

_____

_____

_____

_____

cardiopulmonary resuscitation (CPR)?

_____

_____

_____

_____

Where would you like to receive care?

admission/transfer to hospital?

_____

_____

_____

admission/transfer to ICU?

_____

_____

_____

_____

admission/transfer to a hospice?

admission to a palliative care unit?

After you have died, would you want to:

donate your organs (if possible, depending on the disease process going on within you)?

have an autopsy?

Be buried or cremated?

It is important, perhaps even imperative, that you give a copy of your advance directive to your physician, and that you discuss the contents and the spirit of the contents with your doctor as well as with your health-care proxy (discussed further below). It is also of value to discuss its contents with friends and family who will be involved in providing care for you should it be necessary to do so. That is especially true if it is expected that some of the support group might feel differently than you do about the choices you are making.

Do you have a health-care proxy or a durable power of attorney (someone to make decisions for you in the event you cannot) or a living will (which states what type of treatment you would like to have or refuse to have, given various health situations)? Someday someone may need to speak for you or make decisions on your behalf. Who is most capable of acting as your advocate? Who is most capable of thinking like you do and taking action accordingly? Who is most capable of giving voice to your wishes about end-of-life care? This could be a friend rather than a family member. In fact, some people choose a family member as a matter of loyalty when a friend might be better.

Advance directives are legal in every state in the U.S., though laws in each state can vary. They are also legal in most provinces in Canada. Do you know the laws in your state or province pertaining to advance directives, health-care proxies and living wills? Who might help you get this information?

Does your doctor have documentation regarding your advance directives? Have you spoken with your physician about your advance directive? Does your doctor understand your wishes so that she will be able to act on your behalf in a way that would be respectful of you? Does your doctor know who your health-care proxy is? Has your doctor met this person? Do your family and friends know and understand your wishes as stated in your advance directive? Do they know who your health-care proxy is?

This whole process might be very new for you. If it is, there is value in discussing how you make these decisions. Who do you include in making decisions? Again, at the end of this discussion, the facilitator goes around the circle, asking each person whether he or she has anything to add.

d. Describing What Quality of Life Means to You

Write this title on the flip chart. At this juncture, consider your quality of life—physical, emotional, mental, spiritual, financial and social. This is often the most difficult and challenging part of the process. Frankness and honesty are especially important here. Only you can define or describe what "quality of life" means to you. Your definition might be very different, not only from how those in the room feel, but also from your own definition in the not-too-distant past. That is one of the reasons this process is important. It gives you the opportunity to let other people know your wishes.

What is important to you at this time in your life? What would "quality of life" mean if you had five years of life left? (Five years seems like forever for most people. To imagine that you only have six months to two years of life remaining is more difficult.) What does quality of life mean to you if your life expectancy is two years? Six months or less? A few weeks?

....
....
....
....
....
....

You likely have a sense of what is important to you and how you define your quality of life at present. To discuss quality of life in a five-year context is very different from discussing that topic in a five-week context. If the time that you have been given is short, it is important to set priorities regarding your wishes.

What is the quality of life you have at present in comparison to the quality of life you enjoyed before your illness started? Your answer might help others understand the changes in your life and might also provide a reference point as to how quickly changes are taking place.

....
....
....
....
....
....

In my experience, this is where the group can differ in perspective. In some instances, the patient has begun a process of confronting mortality, while friends and family members still hope for a cure and don't want to address end-of-life issues.

Therefore, at least one or two people need to know your decision-making background and be willing to back you up. So encourage discussion, invite people to ask questions, and express what they can do to help you achieve your goals—but make sure the goals you choose are what *you* want.

Up to this point, we have been reviewing your past, your choices for medical treatment, and your wishes for the time you have left. Now, the discussion moves toward the reality of your life.

What is realistic? What is desirable? What is possible? How much energy do you have on a daily basis? What time of the day do you usually have the most energy?

_____

_____

_____

_____

_____

How has your definition of "quality of life" changed with the knowledge that you have a terminal illness? What brings meaning to your life?

_____

_____

_____

_____

_____

_____

_____

Consider your physical, social, psychological and spiritual well-being. What has sustained you emotionally and spiritually in the past? What sustains you at present?

....

....

....

....

....

....

....

Are there circumstances under which you would consider stopping all medication or treatment? Given the preferences you have expressed, which of the goals you have are feasible, and how might they best be achieved?

....

....

....

....

....

As this part of the meeting draws to a close, the facilitator asks if anyone has anything to add before moving on to the next section.

e. Assessing Practical Considerations

Add this title to the flip chart. The facilitator continues to raise issues and ask questions: Do you have one health-care provider who acts as an advocate for you? Do you have some-one who understands you and works with you? If not, is there anyone in the group who knows of such a person? If so, how might you be linked to that health-care provider? If not, are there other people you could ask in order to find someone like that? The greater the ambiguity about the disease process, the more stressful the end of life will be.

Where might you receive care during the course of your ill-ness—at home, in a hospital, in an extended-care facility, in a hospice?

Although care at home is often the first choice, it can be tax-ing on you as well as on your care provider(s). Who are the care providers? Are they professional and part of the health-care system? Are they your family and friends? Are they avail-able? For how long—over what period of time?

BEING TOUCHED, BEING IN TOUCH

The good moments are certainly good, but the bad times can be very bad. It is great to be around for the intimate moments, the meaningful conversations, the time of shared quiet. It is more difficult during times when pain is poorly controlled, when diarrhea means frequent bed and clothing changes, when nausea, vomiting or wretching doesn't end.

What are the financial costs? Are the costs of treatment covered by insurance? If not, what does insurance cover? What about medication throughout the course of your illness? What are other options for payment? In the United States, it is important to ask how Medicare, Medicaid and private insurance differ. Because terms of coverage can change, it is imperative to ask your social worker, nurse, doctor, or case manager to assist you in determining what the costs will be and who will cover them. Can someone at the meeting agree to act as a financial advocate, research the options, and then deal with insurers if that becomes necessary?

How important is the treatment to you? Is it based on a last hope because dying is simply something you're not ready for, or is there a likelihood that the treatment will reverse the disease process or prolong your life? What are the potential benefits, risks and side effects? Where would you have to travel to get treatment? Who might be affected by your choices? How convenient is the location? Do you know of anyone who has received care at that facility? What was her experience? Are there other facilities to be considered? Who in the group can help you gather information about them? What are the resources available for optimal care?

This includes, first, financial resources:

- Is there money available for equipment (e.g., rental of a bed, commode, wheelchair), for assistance (e.g., home-making, nursing care, assistance with activities of daily living) or for care in a particular facility?

What is the response of your health insurance company to your needs, to your desires? Who might help you with the mountains of paperwork your insurance company requests from you, or with the interaction that needs to take place between you and the insurance company? This is only pertinent where you have private insurance—not as common in Canada as in some other countries.

- As you get sicker, you will have less energy for all of this, and your family will want to be with you rather than fighting with an insurance company. Who might help you with the work that needs to be done in order for you to receive the care you will require?

Second, there are emotional resources. The emotional energy of the people providing physical, emotional and spiritual support is a limited resource. It is important for them to be honest and to make commitments only if they are realistic. Some may want to give the idea more thought, and that's all right. Others might want to commit for a shorter period, after which you meet again and review how everyone is doing. At that time, some people may ask for a break to recharge their own batteries. Ask them to speak honestly about their commitments and limitations, and respond in kind. Some people have a tendency to over-commit, and everyone at some point will likely experience a degree of anger, frustration, guilt or fatigue. Some people will remain stoic in the face of tragedy, unwilling to express their true emotions. But if stress is building, it's important to express it. Speaking openly helps everyone come through the experience healthier, stronger and with a better understanding of themselves and one another. The burdens—and the rewards—are being shared.

Third, consider societal resources. In my experience, individuals often worry that someone else, a sicker person, might need the facilities more than they do. That worry increases if your own financial resources are being drained. Be honest about your own needs and the needs of those who are supporting you.

What does the law say about your wishes? This is especially important with regard to euthanasia and physician-assisted suicide. It might be valuable to have a discussion about the topic. Many people want to talk about it, even if it's not an option for them. Physician-assisted suicide and euthanasia are against the law in Canada and in most U.S. states (Oregon is the exception). In Canada, it is against the law to counsel anyone toward either euthanasia or physician-assisted suicide. It is not against the law to discuss the topic.

That ends the series of questions. There may be other topics of interest or concern. The facilitator then invites everyone to make comments. The "to do" list becomes the plan of action.

Once all the topics have been discussed and recorded, look at what needs to be done—review the "to do" list. This might include a visit to another specialist for a second opinion, assistance with carrying out an activity (to go skiing one more time, to visit a friend in another city, to explore alternative therapies), a visit to a potential hospice, or the drafting of a living will. It is important for the facilitator (or, even better, you) to acknowledge the varied emotions triggered by the process. Be honest; talk about your loss of independence, about your appreciation for everyone's efforts. The plan will work better if people don't over-commit. Review each item and ask who will assume responsibility for that task. Write down that person's name next to the item. Set a deadline for each task. Once the list is complete, set up a second meeting. There is often merit in setting priorities or checking the burdens and benefits of each item on the list. Is everyone who might be affected by this overall plan comfortable with it and able to contribute? If not, why not? What needs to change to enable everyone to put the plan into effect? Some people may have to agree to disagree. How much effort (e.g., time, energy, money) will need to be invested to make the specific event happen? What if it cannot happen? What is the desired outcome? How will the person's life be enhanced if the item can be achieved?

People are making a commitment to being involved in caring for you. What will each person do? Are they duplicating services that could be provided within the health-care system? How long will they provide the care they have committed to?

It might be wise to invite people to make a two-, three-, or four-week commitment, at which time they can choose to take a break or to continue for another period of time. (It is better to review people's services on a regular basis than to have someone run out of energy or find that they are unable to keep the commitment they made and are uncertain about informing the rest of the group that they are unable to continue.)

The process you have just completed will enable all the people who attended to feel that they are in touch with you. It might be of value to create a "fan out" list—those who can be on an email group list computer notification, and those who need to be notified by phone.

FIVE

Life Review

Imagine you are driving a car—it is the car of your dreams—a new VW convertible, a Jaguar, a Volvo; a sports car, a van, an SUV, a truck. Whichever car you imagine, it is physically the most comfortable vehicle that you have ever driven.

Next, I invite you to imagine that you are driving along a road that is entirely new to you. You have never been down this road before. Other people have told you about similar roads, and therefore parts of it seem familiar to you, but mile after mile, it is not really known to you. An interesting feature of this road is that while you have a sense of what is in front of you, you are unable to see beyond the front of the car—not because of fog, not because it's dark, or because it's too bright. It is simply a characteristic of the road that you cannot see the next mile, the next distance that you have to travel. How do you feel? Do you experience fear, anxiety, confidence, excitement, trepidation?

A very positive feature of the vehicle you are driving is that the rear-view mirror is very large and allows you to see all that is behind you. Every time you look into that mirror, seeing more and more of what lies behind you helps you to understand where you are going. Some of what you see is beautiful beyond description; some of it seems painful and confusing; some of it is unbearable initially but eventually gives you something that will provide direction for you; some of it is not recognizable. There are other features that put a smile on your face so that you don't ever want to stop looking at that part of the mirror; some of what you see is warming, some of it is chilling, some hopeful, some despairing. As you integrate what you see, you gain wisdom about your journey. You also gain a sense of direction for what lies before you.

Our lives are full of transitions—leaving home, discovering our own values, relocating, choosing a life partner, developing our skills in the work we do, having children, seeing children leave home—our stories are familiar. Part of us dies through each one of those transitions. Then one day we learn about having a terminal illness and our naïveté about life as we know it ends. Dying becomes part of our reality. We can't go back. We move through those transitions and changes to a new way of being, a new understanding of ourselves, of our community, and perhaps even of the world.

Kierkegaard said that "life can only be understood backwards; but it must be lived forwards." There is a benefit to looking in the rear-view mirror as you drive: You see where you have been, and what is approaching from behind—all while you're driving forward. Perhaps one of the best ways to know where we are headed is to make sense of the past, of all that lies behind us. Reviewing one's life is a spontaneous process that begins once people *know* they are dying, once they *know* they have a terminal illness. It seems to be inevitable.

When facing the anxiety associated with a terminal illness, there is value in developing a plan for your care, as was discussed in the previous chapter. And through the process of a life review, you might consider the meaning in your life. Finding meaning may diminish the anxiety you are experiencing and create a degree of certainty for you.

A "life review" simply means that you take time to look at the past while living in the present. It enables you to reconsider life events, relationships, successes, failures. It may also remind you of conversations and activities that might still be desirable. The more this contributes to a sense of certainty about your life, the less anxious you will feel. Life review begins with remembering and reflecting on the past—the choices you've made, your sense of self, your relationships with others, and your connection to a higher power such as God. This type of reflection leads to a range of insights and emotions. The probity—that is, the goodness—in your life can result in a sense of affirmation, accomplishment and contentment. In contrast, if you remember features of your life as tragic, negative or evil, you may experience feelings of guilt, anxiety and depression. It may be a great challenge to make sense of the life you have lived, to find meaning and purpose in your own history. Through that process you might recognize the need to resolve issues within yourself or with another person. You may also come to a new or deeper understanding of events and relationships that were part of your life.

If we do not examine the past, its burdens will weigh us down and impede our ability to make choices for the future. In fact, as philosopher George Santayana said, "Those who cannot remember the past are condemned to repeat it."

Conducting a life review and speaking about it to another person can begin the process of understanding and finding meaning in your own life. It may also serve to reduce the pain and grief associated with some life experiences.

The process is that of reflecting on one's life, one's personal history. It begins from within, and it bursts into our thoughts and dreams. Some people blurt out their life story in conversation. They want their story, their legacy, to be heard. It is more than merely remembering or reminiscing. It is a process by which they make sense of their past with the desire to understand who they are, find meaning in who they have been, and hope for the future.

As gerontologists Gary Kenyon and William Randall write in *Restorying Our Lives*, "Ultimately, the richest resource for meaning and healing is one we already possess. It rests (mostly untapped) in the material of our own life story, in the sprawling, many-layered text that has been accumulating within us across the years, weaving itself in the depths of, and as, our life."

It seems that for most people a life story, or life review, includes a component of grief. It also contains love, joy, gratitude, pride, laughter and hope. For some, it includes guilt and shame.

How do you conduct a life review? For those with a terminal illness, the process may already have begun, as it seems like a natural outgrowth. Two gerontologists, James Birren and Donna Deutchman, authors of *Guiding Autobiography Groups for Older Adults,* have developed a useful structure for the process of life review. It also provides guidance for people who do not have a terminal illness but are trying to make sense of their lives or find meaning in their past. I have adapted their work and incorporated the nine themes they developed for the guided autobiography. You might take pencil and paper in hand to reflect about your own life. You may also choose to record your story on a tape.

Each of the themes of the life review will include a statement and a set of questions that serve to stimulate thought and self-reflection. If you are writing or thinking about your life, you might consider doing so in a place where you will not have any interruptions. You may experience some very happy memories. You may also experience some painful emotions and on that basis decide to speak to someone (a close friend, a counselor, a therapist, a spiritual leader) about your life review process. The insights of others may be of value to you in understanding yourself. As you look back, work to be aware of the emotion(s) you experience throughout the process.

1. Major Branching Points

Life might be regarded as a branching tree, a flowing river, or a trailing plant that puts down roots in various places as it grows. Branching points are the events and inner processes that shape our lives in significant ways. These might include major events such as marriage, commitment to a long-term relationship, relocation, or retirement, or minor events such as reading a book, having a conversation with a close friend or perhaps even a stranger, or going on a vacation.

List five major branching points in your life.

1. _____

_____

_____

2. _____

_____

_____

3. _____

_____

_____

4. _____

_____

_____

5. _____

_____

_____

You might choose one or two of those points to consider in greater detail. Learning that one has a serious or a terminal illness is certainly a major branching point. You may choose to answer these questions using your diagnosis as a major branching point, or you might choose other branching points you experienced in your lifetime.

_____

_____

_____

_____

_____

_____

....
....
....
....

When did these branching points occur?

....
....
....
....

How did they affect your life at the time that they happened? How do you see their effect on you now?

....
....
....
....
....
....
....
....

Who were the significant people involved in these branching points? What role did they have? What effect did the event(s) have on them?

....
....
....
....
....

....
....
....
....

What were the feelings that you experienced at the time of each branching point?

....
....
....
....
....
....
....

What are your feelings about those experiences now?

....
....
....
....
....
....

Did you have a personal choice in how the events unfolded at any branching point?

....
....
....
....

....

....

What were the immediate consequences of the events that formed the branching point? What were the long-term consequences?

....

....

....

....

....

....

....

....

What might your life be like if this branching point had not occurred?

....

....

....

....

....

....

....

....

If you are completing this and have a terminal illness, how does the event you have just been thinking about compare to learning about having a terminal illness?

How specifically has your life changed since you learned about your illness?

----

2. Family of Origin and Adult (or Chosen) Families

Your family of origin is determined by your birth or adoption. We don't have a choice about our family of origin. The people we grow up with make a significant contribution to who we become as adults. As adults we have the opportunity to choose our families—our spouses, partners, other people we live with, and those we choose to share our lives with in an intimate way. I learned while working in palliative care that "family" can be defined in many, many different ways.

How do you define family for yourself?

....
....
....
....
....
....

Who is in your family of origin (grandparents, parents, siblings, aunts and uncles)? Sometimes close friends are regarded as aunts and uncles. You may choose to include such people in your family of origin. Did the members of your family of origin live near you? How much time did you spend with these people?

....
....
....
....
....
....
....

Who is in your adult family (your family of choice)?

....
....
....
....
....

Which family members played a role in shaping your life—in a positive way, in a negative way? Try to think of specific events that demonstrate the role they played in shaping your life, in either a positive or a negative way.

....

....

....

....

....

....

....

....

What would I need to know about your family of origin to understand who you are?

....

....

....

....

....

....

....

....

What would I need to know about your family of choice to understand who you are?

....

....

....

....

....

....

....

....

....

....

Who held the power in your family of origin? How did that affect you? How did that influence who you are today? Who holds the power in your adult family?

....

....

....

....

....

....

....

....

Who made the decisions, and how were decisions made? Who makes the decisions in your present family? How are they made?

....

....

....

....

....

How was affection expressed in your family? How is affection expressed in your present family? Are members of your family comfortable with touch (hugs), either being touched (hugged) or touching (hugging) others?

What were the areas of conflict? What are current areas of conflict? What were the areas of conflict before you or a family member received a diagnosis of a terminal illness?

How was conflict resolved? Do you work toward resolving conflict in your family of choice? How do you do it? How is this process informed or affected by the way conflict was resolved in your family of origin?

....

....

....

....

What were the family rules in your family of origin? Were they talked about or were you simply expected to know them? What was the source of the rules?

....

....

....

....

....

....

....

....

Who loved you in your family of origin? Who did you love in your family of origin? Who loves you in your adult family (family of choice)? Who do you love in your adult family?

....

....

....

....

....

....

....

How did you experience that love? How do you experience their love as an adult? How do you demonstrate your love to family members? How do you let them know that you love them?

What were the strengths and weaknesses of your family of origin?

What are the strengths and weaknesses of your adult family?

....

....

....

....

....

....

....

....

What are some of your favorite family (of origin or adult) memories?

....

....

....

....

....

....

....

....

....

What are some of your painful family (of origin or adult) memories?

....

....

....

....

....

....

....

....

....

....

What events have torn your family (either your family of origin or your family of choice) apart, or strengthened the family?

....

....

....

....

....

....

....

....

What are your family (of origin or adult) secrets? What effect did they have on you as you were growing up? What effect do they have on you as an adult?

....

....

....

....

What was and is your relationship to your parents?

Who are the significant family members in your life at present, especially in the context of your illness?

....
....
....
....
....

Who would you like to have present through the last days and weeks of your life? What are the reasons you would like those people present?

....
....
....
....
....
....
....
....
....
....
....

Who would you like to have present at the time of your death?

....
....
....
....
....
....

....

....

....

....

Often, one's life story is divided between love and work. Love pertains to the personal part of life, the relationships with family members and friends. Work pertains to one's job, one's profession, one's productivity.

3. Career or Major Life's Work

A career is a major life's work. It takes up your time and energy. Often we think of it as the work we do outside the home for pay. It might also include what we do in a relationship, for example, in being a parent, a partner, a husband or a wife. Work may also include a special interest such as art, music, or education; or working as a volunteer in community service.

What is—or was—your career? Perhaps you had more than one. Feel free to list as many as you would like to list.

....

....

....

....

....

....

....

....

How did you come to choose your career(s)?

_____

_____

_____

_____

_____

_____

As a child, what did you want to be when you grew up? How did that change over time? Did some individual or circumstance influence your choice?

_____

_____

_____

_____

_____

_____

What have the benefits, hurdles, and surprises been within your career(s)?

_____

_____

_____

_____

_____

_____

Do you wish you had made a different choice? Or do you wish you had made the choices you made at a different time of your life?

If you had several careers, how did that come about? What were the circumstances around the career changes that took place? Do you have regrets about those changes? If so, what are they? How might your life be different if you had stayed with a particular career?

What do you consider the successes and failures in your work? What parts of your work are you most proud of? Are there any parts of your work that you would like to forget?

What were the most enjoyable and least enjoyable aspects of your work? What are some of the specific memories around these aspects of your work?

Which feature of your career do you most celebrate? What features of your career(s) do other people most celebrate?

If you did it all again, what would you do differently? Would that have been possible at the time? How do you feel about that now?

_____

_____

_____

_____

_____

_____

_____

_____

_____

Depending on the age at which you became ill, do you experience a sense of loss with regard to your career?

_____

_____

_____

_____

_____

_____

_____

_____

Are there things you would still like to do, or to have done, before you stop working? What are they?

_____

_____

_____

_____

....
....
....
....

4. The Role of Money

Money is an important theme in life. It affects many aspects of our lives: family, education, career, relationships, activities and self-esteem. Attitudes toward money are affected by a variety of positive and negative influences.

Was money talked about in your family? Did someone teach you about money—if so, who and how? If you have children, what have you taught them about money?

....
....
....
....
....

What role did money have in your family of origin? Did your parents or others worry about money? Was money the focus of conversation? If so, in what regard?

....
....
....
....

Were you poor, or financially secure, and what impact did that have on you as a child and as an adult? Did anyone take risks with money? What effect did that have on your family? Were there sudden losses or gains with regard to money or income?

How have you made or received money as an adult? How important has money been to you as an adult? Are you satisfied with the amount of money you have or the potential amount of money you could receive?

What was the biggest financial mistake you made, and what was your greatest financial success?

_____

_____

_____

_____

_____

_____

_____

Are your financial affairs in order? If not, how do you feel about that? What would need to be done in order to get them in order? Who might assist you in that regard?

_____

_____

_____

_____

_____

_____

_____

Who knows about your money? Who needs to know about your money? What do they need to know?

_____

_____

_____

Are you generous or stingy with money?

Have you managed your money well or poorly? How do you feel about how you have managed your money? Does it affect your self-esteem?

How does having a terminal illness affect your attitude toward money? For example, how do you feel about the money you earned, and the money you saved, now that you have a terminal illness?

....
....
....
....
....
....

How is the way you think about or manage your money similar to the way your parents thought about and managed money? How is the way you feel about money similar to the way your parents felt?

....
....
....
....
....
....
....

How does your way of thinking about or managing money differ from that of your parents?

....
....
....
....
....
....

If you had your life to live again, what would you do differently or similarly with regard to money?

What will you do with your money before you die—and after you are gone?

Have you named someone as your power of attorney? If not, who might you choose? What does this person need to know about your financial and business affairs?

....

....

....

....

Do you have a will? If so, is it current? Has anything changed since you learned that you have a terminal illness? Who has been named as the executor? Does this person know where the will is? Does the will include wishes you might have with regard to a funeral, memorial service, wake, celebration of life?

....

....

....

....

....

....

....

5. Health and Body Image

Your overall health and body image are a complex and significant part of who you are. There are objective features that make up who you are physically, and there are subjective features that contribute to how you feel about yourself—your self-image. Self-image often involves comparing oneself to others in terms of appearance, strength, frequency of illness, physical ability and attractiveness. Consider those features through your lifetime, beginning in infancy and moving through childhood, adolescence, and early, middle and late adulthood.

How would you describe your body?

What part of your body do you like the most?

What parts of your body are characteristic of your mother's side or your father's side of the family? If you were adopted, would you like to have that information?

What part of your body do you like least?

If you could change one feature of your body, what would it be? Have you ever had a body part changed? What was the process of making the change? How did the change affect you?

_____

_____

_____

_____

_____

Does all or part of your body embarrass you? Has anyone every teased you or poked fun at you because of a body part? How did you respond? What effect did that have on you after the event?

_____

_____

_____

_____

_____

How has your body changed through the course of your present illness?

_____

_____

_____

_____

_____

How do you feel about your body since you learned about having a terminal illness? Do you feel betrayed by your body, or by a particular body part?

_____

_____

_____

_____

_____

_____

_____

6. Sexual Identity, Sex Roles and Sexual Experiences

Sexuality includes our sense of sexual identity, that is, of being male or female; our thoughts, ideas and practices regarding sex role behavior; and our sexual experiences.

Do you remember when you first learned about being a boy or a girl? Were you with someone at the time? What were the circumstances surrounding that awareness?

_____

_____

_____

_____

_____

_____

_____

_____

_____

What toys, games and activities made up your play as a child?
Of those, which were your favorites? Did any of them become
hobbies in your adult life? Did you spend time playing with
siblings, with friends or on your own?

_____

_____

_____

_____

_____

_____

_____

_____

Was anything forbidden?

_____

_____

_____

_____

_____

_____

_____

How did/do your parents view your sexuality? Did they ever speak to you about their view of your sexuality?

How did/do your siblings view your sexuality? Did they ever speak to you about their view of your sexuality?

Where and from whom did you get your sex education? How did the information you were given affect your first sexual experiences? What do you wish you had known at the time of your first sexual experiences?

What were your sexual experiences like, beginning in childhood and moving into adolescence and adulthood?

This may be a particularly difficult question to answer. Have you ever had a traumatic sexual experience?

....

....

....

If so, how did it happen and who was involved? What was lost through that experience? What have you done about it? Are there unresolved issues regarding the event? If so, who might be able to help you work through these issues?

....

....

....

....

....

....

....

....

....

How would you define the "ideal" relationship? Has that been your experience? Do you know of anyone who is living in that ideal?

....

....

....

....

....

....

....

....

What does being feminine mean to you? What does being masculine mean to you? Do you have role models in that regard? Who might they be?

_____

_____

_____

_____

_____

_____

_____

_____

How do you relate to members of the same sex and those of the opposite sex? Are you more comfortable with one or the other?

_____

_____

_____

_____

_____

_____

_____

7. A Lifetime of Loves and Hates

Love and hate are powerful emotions. Love is a strong emotional attachment to a person, place or thing, and hate is a strong feeling of dislike or animosity toward a person, place or thing.

What have been the major loves and hates in your life (persons, places, ideas, behaviors, things)? What are you aware of emotionally as you remember those loves and hates?

What were your loves and hates during your childhood, adolescence and adulthood? Has the knowledge that you have a terminal illness changed your perspective on the loves and hates of your lifetime? If so, how?

Were you allowed to express love and hate throughout your lifetime? If so, how did you express these emotions? If not, what effect did that have on you?

_____

_____

_____

_____

_____

_____

_____

_____

Have you lost a love, or learned to appreciate something or someone you once hated? How did that happen?

_____

_____

_____

_____

_____

_____

_____

What does intimacy mean to you today? With whom do you share this type of intimacy? With whom would you like to share this type of intimacy?

_____

_____

_____

_____

_____

_____

_____

_____

_____

Have you ever been consumed by love or by hate? How did that affect your sense of self? How did this affect your relationship with the person you loved or hated?

_____

_____

_____

_____

_____

_____

_____

_____

_____

Have you ever disliked someone so much you wished they would die?

_____

_____

_____

_____

_____

_____

Knowing you have a terminal illness, do you think there is something left to do with regard to the loves and hates in your life? How might that come about?

....

....

....

....

....

....

....

....

....

....

8. Experiences of Death and Ideas about Dying

Death affects people in many ways. Some people might consider any major loss as a death. Others regard death only as the death of another person. You may have experienced the death of a pet in your childhood. You may also have experienced the death of a family member (grandparent, parent, spouse, sibling, child), a friend, a hero. And you may presently be experiencing your own process of living with a terminal illness. Your previous experience (pets, friends, family members) of dying and death will likely have an effect on your own process of coming to the end of your life. I suggest that you contrast your previous experience with your present experience. This might be a very difficult section to work on. You will likely experience a deep sense of grief and loss. As suggested earlier, it may be of value to speak with someone about your feelings and your experiences and ideas around dying and death.

What is your first memory or first experience of death?

....
....
....
....
....
....
....
....
....
....

How have your experiences and thoughts about death affected who you are? How has that contributed to your present experience?

....
....
....
....
....
....
....

....
....
....
....

Have you ever felt abandoned by someone who died? Have you ever felt abandoned by the death of a pet? Some people regard pets as the perfect companions, loyal friends that have shared many important landmarks or significant events. For some people, their relationship with their pet might be more significant than any relationship they have with another person.

....
....
....
....
....
....
....

How was death talked about or experienced in your family of origin? How about in your adult family?

....
....
....
....
....
....
....

Grief might be defined as wanting more of what one will never get again. How have you grieved with regard to death or loss?

Have you experienced a death or a loss that you have yet to grieve? How might that come about?

What role, if any, has war played in your life? Were you involved in war in any way, which includes being a peacekeeping soldier? Were either of your parents involved in a war? How did that affect your childhood or your relationship with that parent? Were either of your parents conscientious objectors? Have you had a sibling go to war? In considering the question of war in your life, you could go back another generation to ask whether any one of your grandparents was involved in the war. How did that affect your parents and subsequently how did it affect you?

Have you ever killed someone?

What were the circumstances? How did you feel about it at the time?

How does that compare to your current feelings about the event?

Try to recall the first funeral you ever attended. What is the most significant component of that memory? How did it affect you?

How has your previous experience regarding death and dying affected your current experience of knowing that you have a terminal illness?

Is the experience changing and, if so, how?

How would you like to die?

Do you have fears about dying? What are they? That could include the physical process of dying, the sense that it is something you do alone even though you may not be alone, and/or the questions or sense you have about life after death.

Do you have fears about being dead? Are you able to name the fears?

....

....

....

....

....

....

....

....

....

If you could ask a dead person one question about the dying process, what would it be?

....

....

....

....

....

....

....

9. Life Goals and the Meaning of Life

Meaning, values and purpose in life are often difficult to describe or speak about. The simplicity of childhood—right and wrong, black and white, true and false—changes to shades of gray and uncertainty in adulthood. Some people find comfort in religion or other spiritual practices.

How do you define spirituality? How do you define religion? What do they mean to you? What are your practices in that regard?

_____

_____

_____

_____

_____

_____

_____

_____

_____

_____

_____

What was the religious tradition in your childhood, in your home, in your community? What are the religious traditions in your adult life?

_____

_____

_____

_____

_____

_____

_____

_____

Have you ever had a religious/spiritual experience?

How did that experience come about?

What were the immediate and long-term effects? How important is that experience to you today? Has its importance changed with the knowledge that you have a terminal illness?

Are there symbols in your life that are important to you? How did they come to be meaningful to you? How do you incorporate them into your life?

_____

_____

_____

_____

_____

_____

_____

_____

_____

_____

What principles guide your life? What is the basis of these principles? How did they come to be important to you?

_____

_____

_____

_____

_____

_____

_____

_____

_____

How does nature fit into your understanding of meaning or spirituality? If possible or pertinent, describe a setting in

FACING DEATH, EMBRACING LIFE

nature that gives you meaning or a deep sense of connection to something greater than yourself.

_____

_____

_____

_____

_____

_____

_____

What has given your life meaning in the past? What gives your life meaning at present?

_____

_____

_____

_____

_____

_____

_____

Have there ever been times when your life felt meaningless? What did you do to get through that time, if anything? Was there anyone who was particularly important to you at that time?

_____

_____

_____

....

....

....

....

....

....

....

How has your sense of spirituality changed since you learned about having a terminal illness?

....

....

....

....

....

....

....

Some people will find that it is painful to complete a life review, especially as they experience grief that has been unexpressed through the course of their lifetime. For some, it is valuable to do this work in a group or to get the help of another individual who is willing to support you through the process. At a time in my life when I was filled with grief, I was given a valuable piece of advice: Express your sorrow with another person, a trusted friend. Repeat your story with all the emotion it involves until your friend fully understands you, your story and your grief.

As one goes through the process of a life review, unexpected emotions will likely be aroused—despair, hopelessness, anger, rage, sadness. For some, these emotions can be overwhelming. If that is the case, contact a friend or family member who will respect emotion without judgment. Ask the person to respond only with questions for clarification. It is important to state that you remember a tragedy, and in remembering you are experiencing a very powerful emotion. Invite the person to be with you. Then, in great detail, remember the event, the person, the loss. Include the features and characteristics that you value. Stay in the emotion until it comes to resolution. Some people might benefit by contacting a professional counselor if this emotion is severe and does not subside.

Often those who review their lives come to appreciate the meaning and purpose of their lives in a new way. Some will remember the wisdom and compassion that emerged in their lives through various experiences. Perhaps through the process conflicts have been resolved, new insights about who they are have been gained, and relationships with loved ones have been strengthened. Hopefully in looking back, people will live forward with a renewed purpose, sense of direction, and commitment to those they love.

SIX

Truth

Knowing that one has a terminal illness may serve as a catalyst for seeking, understanding and speaking one's truth. Questions previously ignored now linger in one's thoughts. *Who am I? How did growing up in my family of origin affect who I am today?* and *What is my unfinished business with regard to who I am in the world?* are a few examples of such questions. People think about their past and present relationships, their sense of purpose, value and meaning, and their sense of connection to the universe, to all of time and space, to God. It seems that people with a terminal illness have a deep desire to know themselves and to be known by others.

You might complete the next exercise before you go on reading. Draw another timeline, or perhaps you would prefer to work with one of the timelines you have already drawn. Place an X one centimeter from the right end of the line: Extend a dotted line beyond the word Death.

Birth————————————————*X—Death* - - - -

Imagine that the time that remains for you is approximately six months. Write your name below the X. What do you feel as you write your name?

_____

_____

_____

_____

Name some people that you love and/or care about and with whom you have some unfinished business. You might write their names above the X. You may even be estranged from these people at present. One or more of these people may no longer be physically part of your life. They may have moved away, or perhaps they died, and yet the unfinished business is still with you.

1. _____
2. _____
3. _____
4. _____
5. _____
6. _____

Remember a time when you were in a close(r) relationship with each of those people. Think about a particular event that symbolizes that closeness, or think about one of your favorite memories of this person.

_____

_____

What was the event or what were the words that ruptured the relationship?

In an ideal world, what would you like to say to this person? What would you like them to understand about you? What, if anything, would you like to hear from them?

What would your life be like if you were able to take care of this unfinished business?

How might this come to be? Is there anyone who could facilitate a conversation between the two of you? Who would that be? If the person has died you might consider writing them a letter or imagining that you are speaking to them.

Think about the person you have just written about. How might the ruptured relationship have affected them? Will this effect continue after you die? What gift might you be giving this person by addressing the issue between you?

Anne had unfinished business with her daughter. I entered Anne's room while doing my Saturday morning rounds, as I wanted to check with her about her pain. Her daughter, Kathy, was sitting at the foot of the bed. Anne and I spoke about her pain. She was pleased and relieved to finally be free of the discomfort. While talking about the relief, she began to cry. I was surprised to see her cry and invited her to speak about her tears.

Looking at me, she said, "I want to say that I have not been a very good mother." What a painful and yet courageous thing to say! It was followed by silence. Anne continued to cry, as did Kathy. She had tears streaming down her face. I asked Anne to speak directly to Kathy, giving her eye contact as she said to Kathy exactly what she had just said to me. Kathy seemed not to want to hear what her mother had to say—it was painful for both of them.

Anne looked at Kathy and said:

You know when you were five years old, you begged to take ballet lessons. We couldn't afford those lessons—it would have meant a long drive into town, which would have taken me away from the work on the farm, and we just didn't have the money to be able to let you take those lessons. But all our neighbors who had little girls made the effort and provided that for their daughters. I have great regrets about not making that happen for you and I feel like I was not a good mother.

Anne had just spoken about a burden she had carried for twenty-nine years. Kathy looked at her mother and without missing a beat stated, "I might not know how to dance as a ballerina, but how many of my childhood friends or adult colleagues know how to lasso a calf?" The tears changed to smiles, followed by chuckles. I stepped out of the room. They continued to speak for several hours. Shortly after her conversation with Kathy, Anne invited her children to come from various parts of the United States. She had something to say to each one of her children.

Once Anne was free of physical pain, she was able to address her emotional pain. In a sense, you might say, she stepped into it. She made the choice to talk about her despair. This resulted in changing what seemed to be a failure into a celebration. She could have chosen to keep silent, to contain her despair, but in expressing the despair her pain took on new meaning—not only for her, but also for Kathy. As is true of anyone with a terminal illness, Anne might have felt that the real opportunities of life had passed her by. But dying created new opportunities. Twenty-nine years after the fact, Anne was finally able to describe the scenario and speak her truth.

Anne's truth consisted of the facts as she remembered them, the feelings as she had experienced them, and her judgment of being a woman who had not been good enough as a mother. Her truth carried with it a sense of failure. It was spoken to Kathy, one of only a few people who could say whether Anne's truth was her truth as well. Finally, Anne was free of the isolation, the sense of failure and the self-judgment. The part of her that died twenty-nine years earlier was restored and reintegrated into her being. She would die with less despair and greater integrity.

As much as there is light in our stories, so there is also darkness and shadow. Only by embracing the darkness can we step into a new light. In speaking her truth, Anne changed her life's course as well as that of her daughter. By introducing a topic that had been a concern for her for decades, she paved the way for a deeper relationship with her daughter and subsequently with her other children. Not only would that alter the degree of intimacy between them and amongst them while she was alive, it would likely also diminish the depth of the grief her family members would experience following Anne's death.

Truth has to do with telling your personal story. Anne was able to speak about her life as she really experienced it. She no longer kept her truth a secret. Individuals, families, groups and organizations all keep secrets. In turn, secrets keep individuals, secrets keep families, secrets isolate and hold their keepers hostage. Essentially, people keep secrets and secrets keep people. If those secrets are linked to guilt and shame, they are all the more powerful in their ability to isolate and silence the secret-keepers, to prevent them from speaking the truth.

Intimacy is based on clear and honest communication

(by word, behavior and touch), as well as attentive listening. In this way, safety, trust and inclusion are established. Each person is wholly appreciated for who the person really is.

As we confront our own reality, we may gain understanding and insight about who we are. Our disguises of the past begin to be diminished. If, through that process, we discover that we have hurt or damaged another person, we must apologize. This will help to free us from old, unconscious and unjustified feelings of guilt that may stem from our past, beginning in childhood. If we don't do this work; if we don't address our wrongdoings and act to correct them, feelings of guilt may persist.

Guilt results from having committed an offence against civil or religious law or the unwritten rules of human relationships. Guilt triggers the conscience. It is a healthy mechanism, a signal to pay attention to an action that may have hurt another person, a reminder to act responsibly and with integrity. Guilt can also be described as the *feeling* of having committed an offence. It is a response, the belief that we should not have done something, or the belief that we *should* have done something when we did not. Guilt arises from what we do and also from what we do not do.

Feeling guilty is an emotional response to a choice or an action that has violated a relationship or resulted in suffering. Resolution of guilt begins when a person recognizes his error and assumes responsibility for that action and the hurtful consequences that have resulted. Such recognition can occur only after we stop blaming others. Over the course of our lives, we avoid taking full responsibility for our actions for a variety of reasons—fear, the desire to avoid discomfort (emotional pain), indifference. As a result, we live with guilt until something moves us to an awareness of that emotion and a desire to repair the relationship.

The diagnosis of a terminal illness can usher in an overwhelming flood of memories and heightened self-awareness. Many people who become aware of their guilt, work toward resolution. In some instances, they seek forgiveness. Until that happens, they may be preoccupied with thoughts and feelings related to guilt.

James Hollis, a Jungian psychologist, speaks of "recognition, recompense, and release." To those three Rs I add remorse, for it often follows recognition. As people remember their past, they recognize the harm that came to themselves or others because of something they did or did not do. At that point, they can acknowledge the part they played—or they may continue to blame others. But to blame another is to continue living in the cloud of denial; to assume responsibility for the action is to move toward resolution and release, from despair toward integrity. In assuming responsibility for one's actions, there can be a sense of remorse, true regret for whatever one has taken, for the suffering that resulted from words or actions.

Recompense means one returns that which has been taken. Because much of what has been done cannot be undone, it is usually a symbolic return, a gesture of giving back. It is only effective if done with sincerity, and only makes sense in the context of genuine contrition. In the context of a religious perspective, one might seek forgiveness or reconciliation.

On occasion I am asked when it is most appropriate to visit a dying relative. I always advise "sooner rather than later." It is difficult to predict when the illness will begin to hamper meaningful interaction. I usually add that if there is only enough money to make one trip to visit the dying person, go while the person is still alive (i.e., as opposed to attending the funeral). And if you are someone who has a terminal illness and has something to say to another person, I recommend that you arrange a visit as soon as possible. If you are too sick to travel, invite the person over for a visit. If you have the resources, offer to help with travel expenses.

Although the dying process is experienced by the individual, it affects many people. What does or does not happen during the process will affect the grief and mourning of family members and friends. So don't wait! Sometimes there is an urgent need to speak the truth to one another, to understand a past or current relationship, to express the meaning of one's life to another person. For some relationships, that means having courage and taking risks, especially if a wrong needs to be corrected.

Perhaps the recognition that one needs both to be forgiven and to forgive shows us two sides of the same coin. Only in forgiveness can one be freed of the guilt associated with an action.

There are many reasons why it is painful to remember and recognize those acts and omissions in our relationships that caused another person to suffer. These might include a spouse who held the family together emotionally for years without protest or bitterness; the child who carried her parents through alcoholism, mental or physical illness, or financial distress; the sibling who without question or complaint cared for the younger children when the parents were unable to do so.

How does all this become relevant? It has to do with being whole. The life you have lived is part of who you are, your entire life—whether you're proud or ashamed of it or feel guilty about things you've done and wish you had not done. Try to think of the events, relationships and inner processes of the past as fragments of life, your life. Some (perhaps most) of them might be regarded as good, others as bad, and some as ugly or as unacceptable to us. Are you able to hold them in the present? If so, you likely have a sense of wholeness; if not, perhaps yours is a sense of feeling fragmented. Only by integrating all of who you are can you become whole. The word "whole" is related to the German word *heil.* As an adjective it means "all of, entire, in an unbroken or undamaged state; in one piece"; as a noun it means "a thing that is complete in itself." Significantly, the word "heal" has the same origin and means "to cause to become sound or healthy again." It seems that individuals who are able to integrate all of their past into their present experience a sense of healing or wholeness, despite the fact that they are not cured of their illness. These are the people who express thankfulness for learning that they have a terminal illness, despite the fact that they will not experience a cure from their illness, "I will die healed, not cured!"

As you review the events and relationships of your life, what happens when you realize there are things you would like to say to someone, or a truth you would like to talk about? What if you know someone who is dying and would like to say something, or perhaps you would like to hear what that person has to say to you? This may or may not have to do with forgiving and being forgiven.

Appreciate the courage it takes to face the truth of who you are. Recognize your desire for resolution and inner peace. And know that your basic goal is this: to speak the truth as you describe key events and relationships in your life. Be careful to identify any sense of guilt and note what that guilt relates to in your life. In other words, recognize the harm you did to yourself or to another person, and assume responsibility for that harm.

It is not easy to get started, but once you do, it can be a deeply rewarding experience. Some people find that a simple formula makes it easier to say what's on their mind: "I feel [*name the emotion*] because [*state what happened*]." Here's an example: "I feel *great regret* because *I missed your retirement party.*" You might want to add some additional comments such as "We had worked together for twenty-seven years." Another example might be, "I feel *shame and remorse* because *I did not have the courage and knowledge to work through our differences. For that reason we lost a lot of time where we might have been much closer and more supportive of each other.*"

You might speak the truth to another person or write down a description of the event. Follow the facts of the event with a description of the emotions you experienced at the time of the event as well as the emotions you experience as you are remembering the events. Consider what it might mean to forgive someone, to be free of anger and resentment toward that person, or to ask for forgiveness and to be free of guilt.

....

....

....

....

....

....

....

In some instances, especially if life expectancy is short, family members can have difficulty speaking truthfully to a terminally ill relative. How do you break through safe but superficial conversation to a more intimate level? With a little guidance, it can be easier than you think. Let me outline how it could happen.

1. Create a private space. If you are living at home, invite the person to come to your house. Make arrangements for an uninterrupted visit. If you are meeting in someone else's home, ask for privacy until the conversation is complete. If you are meeting at the hospital, find a private space, if possible. If you are a patient in a private room, invite the person you would like to speak with to meet you at the hospital, informing them of your intent to speak about some private matters. Ask the nurse for an hour of privacy with the door closed. Check on whether you will require any medication or other care during that period. Put a "Please do not disturb" sign on the door with the message that private time is required.

2. This is an important time. Make certain that radios, CD players, cell phones, pagers are turned off. Extra noise, pets or

other people can easily distract you from the conversation you want to have.

3. Make certain both of you are physically comfortable, in a position that fosters eye contact and being in touch. Sit near enough to be able to easily and comfortably touch each other. Ask if it's okay to hold hands, if that's best. You could say:

I would like to hold your hand (put my hand on your arm or shoulder) while we speak. Is that all right with you?

4. Be aware of your emotions as you begin. You might say that this is difficult.

I find this difficult to say . . .

I feel a little awkward about this . . .

I don't know how to begin, but I do know that I have something to say to you. I believe this needed to be said long ago.

5. Explain why it is important to speak to one another.

You have always been very important to me . . .

We have always been honest with each other . . .

I have a few things I would like to speak to you about . . .

I want to stop pretending that I might get well again. I know how sick I am. At times that scares me, keeps me awake, and makes me feel very alone . . . I would like you to share this journey with me.

6. Assure the person that you will end the conversation whenever the person wants it to end. Agree that it is not your intention to hurt, but be aware that hurt or pain might occur. If it does occur, agree to work toward resolution:

I do not want to hurt you in any way, but I am aware that some of the things I will say to you might cause some discomfort for both of us.

I would like to know if what I am saying to you is causing you pain. I would also like you to know that if something you say is painful for me to hear, I will let you know.

I don't want you to keep from saying something that you want to say because you think that it might be painful for me to hear. As far as I am concerned, pain is not a reason to keep silent.

7. Begin the conversation. Speak clearly, and slowly. Avoid euphemisms and metaphors. Say exactly what it is you want to say. Because I don't know what it is you want to say to another person, I have included a few examples of how a conversation might begin:

Some of what I have to say is very easy to say. Other parts are more difficult. First, I want you to know how you have influenced my life. I want to remind you of some of the events that were particularly important to me.

I want you to know why I value you, and our relationship.

I want to clear the air between us, as we have always worked hard to be honest with one another. Do you remember the time that . . . ? It affected me for a long time and in some way came between us.

Something that happened some time ago made me very angry. I wish I could have spoken about it earlier, but I was afraid of your reaction. I had two fears: one of being rejected by you for the anger and another that you might be offended, and I didn't want to hurt your feelings. I see now that it would have been better for me to talk about it earlier. It has created a barrier between us. It has compromised our relationship for too long.

I feel that I hurt you when . . . and I'm very sorry about that. Could you forgive me for . . . ? or I felt hurt by you when . . .

I want you to know that I care very deeply about you. I want you to know that I love you.

8. Provide opportunities for the other person to speak as well. As you listen, suspend all judgment.

I'm wondering whether you might tell me what you just heard me say as I want to be absolutely certain that there are no further misunderstandings between us.

I'm sure there must be some things that you want to talk about. I would be very pleased to hear them.

I wonder whether you might want to say some things to me as well. How can I make that easier for you?

9. While the other person is speaking, listen with your full attention. When the person is finished, ask questions for clarification.

If I understand you correctly . . .

Could you tell me more about what you mean, what you feel, or what you think?

Are you saying that . . . ?

Avoid asking questions that begin with "why."

10. Let the other person know how you feel about them. Speak honestly. Don't exaggerate. Keep the conversation simple.

I don't want to say goodbye to you.

I love you.

Your friendship has meant a great deal to me.

As a close family member, you . . .

11. If you sense any agitation or restlessness as you speak, stop. Make statements like:

I sense that you might be uncomfortable about what I just said.

I'm wondering if you have something to say in response to what I just talked about?

Would you prefer to continue this conversation at another time?

I would be interested to hear about how you feel concerning the things I just talked about.

While I sense that you might be a little uncomfortable, I would like to finish this conversation, if that's all right with you.

12. Express gratitude for the time you spent together and arrange for another visit, if desirable.

I appreciate having this chance to talk to you. I would like to talk with you some more. Could we do this again some time?

13. If it is someone you have been estranged from and you feel that you would like to continue spending time together, ask whether the other person feels the same way.

I value the time we spent together today.

I wonder whether we could meet once a week for the next several weeks. That would be very important to me. Would you be interested in doing that?

Is there anything we could do to prevent history from repeating itself? How will we let each other know if we are hurt by something that is said or done?

As we move toward the truth of our experience, we will inevitably learn the value of forgiveness, forgiving others, being forgiven and forgiving ourselves. Forgiveness is not only a word, it is a process. Forgiveness begins by stepping into our emotional pain, by acknowledging what the real issues are and how we feel about them. It means we can no longer deny what happened. We no longer attempt to explain it away or try to understand the other person and why the hurt might have occurred. We no longer pretend it didn't happen, trivialize its effect on us or try to forget it. It means we look at the hurt and its effect on us, that is, we look at what our lives have been like with the hurt; we also look at what our lives would have been like without the hurt. William Meninger, the author of *The Process of Forgiveness* emphasizes the importance of knowing not only whom we forgive, but what it is we are forgiving. What is the extent of the injury? How did it affect our lives at the time? How has it affected our lives since then? What has happened to our trust, our self-esteem, our sense of justice and our ability to feel safe and to relate freely in our world? To acknowledge and experience the hurt, the extent of the hurt and all of the pain associated with it, is the beginning of the process of forgiveness.

Suppose the injury occurred between you and a family member? It may be something that occurred recently or something that occurred many years ago and remains unforgiven.

What was the injury? When did it happen? How?

What did you feel at the time (anger, resentment, guilt, shame)?

What do you feel now? (At times we tend to negate or trivialize our emotions. These emotions must find a place for safe expression. Otherwise, they remain denied, suppressed and/or repressed. According to Meninger, they will find a way to be expressed in other ways such as anger, fear, sarcasm, withdrawal, hostility and self-deprecation. They may also seep out of us through "rage, depression, passive-aggressive behaviors, self-abuse, abuse toward others, an inability to be effective in the world, and the inability to have emotionally intimate relationships.")

....

....

If this injury had not occurred between yourself and this family member how would your life have been different? How
would it be different now?

....

....

....

....

....

....

....

What would your relationship with this family member have
been like if this injurious event had not happened?

....

....

....

....

....

....

....

What characteristics of your relationship did you most value
or treasure?

....

....

....

....

....

....

....

....

If the injury between you were healed what feelings would you have about yourself? What feelings would you have toward your family member?

....

....

....

....

....

....

....

....

I encourage you to express your true emotions just as much as I would encourage you to provide a true description of the events of your life. Some methods of emotional expression benefit from the presence of another person serving as a guide, but others do not. Those that you can do alone include writing a letter; punching a pillow, mattress, or punching bag; screaming in a place where you don't feel inhibited; and physical workouts (running, chopping wood, lifting weights, rowing, etc.).

There are many other approaches that facilitate emotional expression: meditation, visualization, journal writing, dream work, dance, singing, painting, crafts such as pottery and weaving, and playing a musical instrument. Any techniques that bring people to a greater self-awareness, as well as the physical and emotional release in working with the body might be of benefit. These include Rolfing, massage, bioenergetics, and Feldenkrais. For some people, working with a counselor or therapist might also be of great benefit.

The process of self-forgiveness is similar to that of forgiving another person. It begins with acknowledging the truth, by being entirely honest with yourself regarding your actions, your attitudes and your words. Subsequently you take responsibility for what you have done. You don't deny it, trivialize it, ignore it or exaggerate it. Allow all your feelings to emerge. All feelings are important and legitimate to the person experiencing those feelings. Some will be painful: regret, remorse, sorrow, grief, envy, shame, guilt, betrayal, loss, anger. As the deeper feelings emerge, identify how these and other feelings have motivated your behavior and thoughts in the past, resulting in feelings of guilt, self-loathing or self-judging in the present.

Have an open heart and accept yourself. Try to acknowledge the dark emotions as well as the pleasant emotions, remembering that all human emotions contribute to a sense of wholeness and integrity.

Acknowledge how past actions, attitudes and words have affected who you are today.

....

....

....

....

....

....

What would your life have been like if you had made different choices?

....

....

....

....

....

How would you feel?

....

....

....

....

....

How would you be different?

....

....

....

....

....

Life events are like the pieces of a patchwork quilt. Supposing the patches were chosen from the well-known blouses and shirts belonging to different family members, the pieces of material would later trigger different memories for each family member who saw the quilt. Such differences are best seen as enhancing the total picture, as opposed to contradicting or negating the value of each memory. If the quilt were on display over a long period, more of its history would come to light. Meaning is altered over time as understanding is enhanced. How you see your life—remembering events, understanding the importance of your relationships, appreciating the sense of meaning you gain in knowing who you are—all this is *your* story, *your* quilt.

Our families are like that quilt. Each of us sees and experiences something unique to who we are. Whenever a child is born or adopted into a family, it is a different family. The dynamics change immediately. And each child will have a unique experience with the same parents. In fact, those parents are not quite the same as before the child was born; there is an additional responsibility to which they must now respond. Also, their relationships with each child are different. Whether within the family or outside it, no two relationships are alike.

Your recollection of the events is your truth. Others might remember events and relationships differently. However, your truth, your recollection, is essential to knowing yourself and to assuming responsibility for the action or the event. Some memories can be exhilarating, satisfying and factual; others can be devastating. When you come up against a devastating memory, you might feel like returning to denial, living as though the memory were not part of your reality. But remember, that makes change impossible; it ties you to the past.

Assuming responsibility for your actions is the key to compensation for the injury or insult you experienced or caused someone else. This is true for those who know they have a terminal illness, as well as for those who are in good health. If assuming responsibility for your actions includes another person and you are able to contact that person, ask to speak to them. As stated earlier, have the conversation in private, in a place where you will not be interrupted. Ask them to listen carefully to what you have to say. In some instances, it may be important to tell them that you are truly sorry for what happened between you; ask them to forgive you, if that is the case. This could be followed by asking what would be necessary for reconciliation. I recommend that you practice what you want to say beforehand.

When remorse is genuine and expressed you will experience release. I recommend this process of forgiveness so that the individual is free to live the rest of his or her days in a clear space, not a place of despair.

Despite their desire and need, many people fail to connect with others. This occurs for any number of reasons—fear, discomfort, inability to go out on a limb. As a result, conversations are often restricted to small talk about the weather, sports, current events, food and money.

Remember that people want their families to hear them and to know *their* truth. In all likelihood, their families also have something to say to them. If no one begins to speak the truth, families and individuals are essentially estranged from one another, paralyzed in silence. To end the conspiracy of silence, someone must speak first, either the person with the terminal illness or the family member. People who are dying want to speak and want to be spoken to. Who speaks first is not important; the fact that someone speaks is very important.

Consider a situation in which someone would like to speak with a friend who has a terminal illness. His family and other friends speak only about cures because they feel that speaking about the other possibilities would be an admission of defeat. It is in this way that a conspiracy of silence begins, which in turn means the person who is dying is left alone with their fear and anxiety about what will happen if the disease is not cured.

It is my sense that fear keeps people silent—fear that if they speak the truth to one another, then all hope will be lost. But truth and hope are not mutually exclusive. In fact, in speaking the truth, new hope might emerge. Life is full of multiple hopes, most of which can coexist.

The following story about Keith might show how it is possible to open up the space for one person to be in contact with another. Keith is in his mid-forties and runs a computer business. He and Liz lived together for twenty-four years, but they never had a formal marriage ceremony. They have a seventeen-year-old son and twin girls aged fourteen. Keith's father died of lung cancer seven years earlier. His mother is alive and lives in the same city. He has two brothers, Glenn, who also lives in the same city, and Darryl, a divorced lawyer who lives in the suburbs.

The three brothers get along well. That wasn't always the case, but following the death of their father they decided to work out their differences and try to spend more time together. All three grew up playing hockey; one of them as a teenager had hopes of playing professionally. As adults, they became avid hockey fans. The brothers cheer for different teams and try to get together to watch a game once a week.

Keith was diagnosed just as the Stanley Cup playoffs started. Even though Keith wants to talk with his brothers about it, he doesn't know how to begin the conversation about his terminal illness. His brothers are afraid that speaking about death will make it happen sooner. And for some reason they don't want Keith to know that they think he is dying. So the three men continue to enjoy each other's company and have conversations about hockey.

Rich is one of Keith's closest friends. He watches the occasional hockey game with Keith, Glenn, and Darryl. Rich is very aware of the conspiracy of silence. One day, on his way home from work, he calls Keith to ask whether he can drop by for a short visit. Keith welcomes the company. Liz is still at work, and the kids are involved in after-school activities.

Arriving at Keith's house, Rich knocks on the door and walks in. He enters the living room, where Keith is lying in a rented hospital bed. Keith is reading. He puts the book down and takes off his glasses. They shake hands. Rich grabs a chair, placing it so he can comfortably speak to Keith.

He begins by saying,

Keith, I have something to say to you, that I've wanted to say ever since you got sick.

He continues:

It is my sense that people here are very afraid to speak about what might be happening. I want to respect you, 'cause I care about you. It's for that reason that I've come to say what I need to say. Is that all right? Do you mind if I continue? We're all pretending that you're going to get better. I want to believe that as much as anyone. And I certainly don't want to take any hope away from you. At the same time I've got to tell you that what I see happening to you and what we're pretending is happening to you are very different. And I don't want you to get any sicker before we have a chance to talk. I need you to hear me out. Are you still all right with this?

You've always been a good friend to me. We've had our arguments and our differences. But we have always worked out our differences and agreed to be honest with each other.

What I see, Keith, is that you are getting sicker. You seem to be more tired; you lose your ability to concentrate every now and again; and I see you losing weight. This process isn't just about you. It's about you, Liz, your kids, your family and a few good friends. All of this has happened very fast. And you know, Keith, I have something to say to you. I'm sure everyone else I named also has something to say.

We need to start talking, man, 'cause what happens if you don't get better? What happens if you get so tired you can't talk to us any more? I'll only say this once: Your kids need to hear from you. The rest of us would like to hear from you. And I put money on everybody having something to say to you as well. It's not going to be easy, but it will only get harder as you wait longer. There's a conspiracy of silence. We're behaving as though you don't have a diagnosis of a terminal illness, but you do.

We're acting as though you're the healthy, active jock you always were.

Like you, I hope you get cured. I also hope that you won't have to deal with a lot of pain or any other physical discomfort. I hope that your kids know you love them, that they hear you tell them that, that Liz knows that you love her as well and that you appreciate the last twenty-four years together. I hope she knows how you want to spend your last months, weeks and days. Don't you think she might have something to say to you as well and likely doesn't find it any easier than you do?

And then there's your mom. After your father's death she probably thought that, in time, she would be next and not you. She's got to have something to say to you. You're her kid. You're not supposed to die before her. To her, you're still her freckle-faced kid who became a very successful businessman overnight. And now that kid is dying. That's just not how it's supposed to happen.

So that's the conversation I came here to start. I hope I didn't offend you and, if I did, I have every confidence that we'll work it out. I just couldn't be silent any more. Sometimes I'm scared to look this in the face, but I'm more concerned that someday I'll look back and wish I had said a bunch of stuff I never said, and that I had heard you say some things as well.

Keith was relieved that the conspiracy of silence had been broken and the two men could finally talk about Keith's death and their friendship. They shared specific memories, times when they appreciated the support of the other and episodes of conflict when trust might have been jeopardized. But because of their commitment to friendship, their relationship weathered the storm, and their trust in one another was actually strengthened. And the process began when Rich demanded, in a gentle way, that Keith start speaking the truth.

Ask yourself whether you are maintaining a conspiracy of silence with anyone you know. Is there something that needs to be said or something you would like to talk about, yet you are uncertain about how to proceed? I suggest you write a draft of what you would like to say to that person:

(ruled blank lines)

That is the beginning of having a difficult conversation. The next step might be to arrange to meet with that person to have this talk, thereby breaking the conspiracy of silence.

SEVEN

Longing to Belong

Longing to belong means we want and need to be loved. It is a basic human need. For some people at the end of life, the longing to belong is fulfilled by members of their nuclear family; for others it is fulfilled by members of their nuclear family as well as by other people they choose to be with; and for some it is fulfilled, not by blood relatives but by those with whom they have chosen to share their lives, their intimacy, and their love. Everyone needs to belong at the beginning of life, throughout life and at the end of life. In that context, complex issues may surface at the end of life.

Divide your life into developmental intervals. You could follow the ones listed below or choose your own. You could also use seven-year intervals (0–7, 8–14, 15–21, 22–28, etc.). Name two or three people who were important to you in each interval, particularly with regard to your sense of belonging. Who loved you? How did they love you? How do you know that they loved or love you? How did they influence who you are today?

Are they still important to you today?

Infancy and Early Childhood

_____

_____

_____

_____

_____

_____

_____

Childhood

_____

_____

_____

_____

_____

_____

Adolescence

_____

_____

_____

_____

_____

_____

Early Adulthood

Adulthood

Mid-life

Late Adulthood

....

....

....

....

....

....

....

The psychologist Abraham Maslow described the longing to belong as the human need for love, affection and belonging. He established a hierarchy of need, based on his understanding of actual needs based in the body. The individual longs for affectionate relations with people in general, for a place in the group or family, and will work hard to achieve that place. Without it, the individual will experience "the pangs of loneliness, of ostracism, of rejection, of friendlessness, or rootlessness." The longing to belong is a deep desire; it is the yearning of one person to be attached or connected to another.

Reviewing your responses to the first exercise in this chapter, when in your lifetime did you most feel that you belonged? When, if ever, during your life did you feel lonely, ostracized, rejected, friendless or without roots? Who satisfies your need to belong now?

....

....

....

....

....

....

....

....

....

....

....

People who know they have a terminal illness speak of a desire to be in a relationship. They refer to their family of origin, sometimes with fondness, warmth and love, sometimes with indifference, anger and resentment. They seem to have a desire to understand their relationships with parents, siblings, other relatives or the people they have chosen as their family. Those who have close relationships with their children and grandchildren often have a sense of hope in the legacy that they will leave; those with broken relationships with parents or children long for resolution before death. Resolution can mean restoring communication, re-establishing trust or under-standing and defining the relationship. Sometimes resolution means letting go of one's hopes for a relationship that was desired but never attained.

Are there broken relationships in your family? Do you hope for resolution? What would resolution mean? How might it come to be? Putting aside all blame, what are you willing and able to do to work toward resolution?

....

....

....

....

The human sense of belonging begins at birth. The degree of intimacy between parent and child is experienced through the senses—how the baby is held and caressed, the tone of voice, eye contact—all of which reflect the physical and emotional availability of the parent. This occurs throughout the routine of the day, whether the infant is being fed, bathed, changed or simply held. These features communicate messages of unconditional love or, in contrast, resentment that the needs of the infant must take precedence. It is the emotion with which the care is delivered that transmits the true message from parent to child. Even as the child grows up and begins to understand language, the content of the verbal message is not as important as *how* the message is spoken.

One's longing to belong originates in the initial relationship(s) that one experiences as an infant with the adults who provide care for that infant. Those relationships seem to have imprinting effects that influence relationships throughout one's lifetime. At the end of life, the complex nature of these early relationships seems to resurface. Some people struggle to understand its significance; others choose to ignore or dismiss it. Because of the profound struggle that some people experience with regard to their parent–child relationships, I have included an explanation that I hope will enhance your understanding of them. You, like many people I spoke to, may have the perspective of both parent and child.

Unconditional love is love given to another person without expecting anything in return. In the context of the parent–child relationship, the parent may have expectations with regard to the behavior of the child, but does not expect the child to meet the needs of the parent. Ideally, unconditional love is given to the child regardless of the situation. The child deserves that love simply for being born into the family. In this way, the child develops a strong sense of attachment to the parent. Everyone has physical, psychological and spiritual needs. For example, physical needs include food, clothing and shelter; psychological needs include the sense of self and the relationship to others; spiritual needs include the awareness of and connection to a source of power or strength bigger than oneself. Adults recognize and meet their own needs, the needs of other adults and the needs of children.

Unconditional love is the necessary ingredient for a child to have a secure attachment to his parents. For the child to develop a secure base, the parent must be present and available physically and emotionally. This results in a tremendous challenge for the parent, as there are endless demands on time and energy. If the parent is too busy, damaged emotionally for some reason, or unaware of the child's situation or emotional experience, secure attachment to that parent will be compromised.

How does attachment happen? John Bowlby describes the process as

> the provision by both parents of a secure base from which a child or an adolescent can make sorties into the outside world and to which he can return knowing for sure that he will be welcomed when he gets there, nourished physically and emotionally, comforted if distressed,

reassured if frightened. In essence, this role is one of being available, ready to respond when called upon to encourage and perhaps assist, but to intervene actively only when clearly necessary.

When the child knows that the parent is available, patient, forgiving, accepting of and responsive to his needs, he will have a strong and consistent feeling of security. His attitude toward himself and others will be similar to the attitude that his parents have toward him. This enables the child to explore and discover the self. As a result, he will more likely grow into the adult he really is, as opposed to the adult that the parents want or expect him to be.

It is important to understand one's family of origin. It is also important to understand that meaningful relationships can happen outside that context, such that one's longing to belong can be fulfilled in different ways. That may be a message of pain as much as it is a message of understanding and hope.

The relationships of parents with their children have an intergenerational component. Parents generally treat their children the way their parents treated them. Psychologist Carl Jung sheds some light to this when he states that "children are driven unconsciously in a direction that is intended to compensate for everything that was left unfulfilled in the lives of their parents." James Hollis, a Jungian psychologist, puts it another way. He says that the greatest burden a child must bear is the "unlived life" of the parent. In this way patterns are passed on from one generation to another. One of the greatest challenges for the parent is to be aware of his or her sense of self. Otherwise the unlived life of the parent will be projected onto the child.

Whether it's a profession or education left unpursued, a sports team not joined, a value not expressed, a religious faith unfulfilled, a musical instrument that went unplayed, or travel opportunities missed, the conscious and unconscious desires, attitudes and values of the parent are projected onto the child. Giving the child what the parent never had then becomes the focus of child-rearing. The parent is reacting to his own childhood rather than loving the child with spontaneity and acceptance for who she is and who she will become. In that way, the desires of the parent impede the parent's ability to provide unconditional love. Instead, the parent places a condition on the relationship: in return for the parent's love, the child must become what the parent was unable to become. This will undermine the ability of the parent to provide a secure base for his child and weaken the attachment between child and parent.

How have you lived or how might you be living the unlived life of your parent(s)? How are your children living your unlived life?

Without attachment, one feels abandoned. One longs to belong, to be attached, to be part of a family, group or community. It is a matter of survival as well as emotional development—and this is true at the end of life as much as at the beginning. In fact, once people learn they have a terminal illness, the process of understanding their childhood can become more powerful than ever. And as much as they review past lives, so, too, they seek to understand their relationships with their parents, and the effect those relationships had. You may find that to be true yourself.

When the parent looks at the child with love, the child internalizes the message that he is lovable. This is reinforced by the parent's tone of voice and touch. If, for whatever reason, the parent looks at the child with mixed emotions, indifference or resentment, the child will internalize that message. "I don't know if I am lovable. I'm not wanted. I'm not appreciated." In these circumstances, the child feels insecure. As he matures, his perception of self continues to be affected by the parent's responses.

A consistent and secure childhood results in an adolescent, and later an adult, who has a strong sense of self. By contrast, the insecure child is hampered by an unconscious defensiveness. Information that could potentially change the internal message, and which the child needs to strengthen the sense of self, is excluded. In this way the adolescent loses the opportunity to enhance his sense of being secure. That child, as an adult, will imagine that others are relating to him just as his parents did, even if those individuals treat him completely differently.

Understanding your early relationship with your parents, whether biological or adoptive, can help you understand your relationship with them throughout your lifetime, and especially if you are living with dying. It may also help you understand other intimate relationships you have had throughout your lifetime. You may have wondered about the power of the relationship you've had with your parents and how much it has accompanied you for much of your life. That relationship may still result in some anger, resentment or discomfort.

How has your relationship with your parents evolved—changed over your lifetime? How have other intimate relationships been similar or different?

_____

_____

_____

_____

_____

_____

_____

_____

_____

_____

The longing to belong of the secure child is met primarily within the family of origin. The longing to belong of the insecure child is *not* met within the family of origin. That child will usually seek to belong, either by working harder to meet the expectations of the family of origin or by working to belong in some way to an alternative family. That could be a group of friends, members of a social organization or colleagues at the workplace. Some people will choose isolation rather than risking another difficult or impossible attachment. For these people, the fear of a second rejection limits their relationships with others.

If you have experienced a secure relationship with your parents, it can be difficult to appreciate the fact that other people may not want to be associated with their parents or siblings. However, if your parents have rejected you, you may well appreciate a similarity. Through my research, I learned that some people speak fondly of their parents, others recognize strengths and weaknesses, and a few don't want to speak about their parents at all.

A sense of belonging is heightened for many people who know they have a terminal illness. People yearn for this sense of belonging to their family of origin, as well as to their family of choice (spouse, partner, children, close friends). You may have known for some years that this need was not met in your family of origin, and yet still be secure and satisfied in your other relationships. However, if you have recently come to realize that this need has not been met by your family of origin, you will likely experience a sense of betrayal and pain.

For your own well-being, it is helpful to confront or face pain. In fact, the only way to be free of pain is to move through and beyond it. Work to understand your longing to belong. The need for love and acceptance, if not met by a parent, will motivate a child to seek it elsewhere. It is a powerful force. And unless you face your pain, the search can result in relationships that are no more satisfying than the relationship with your parents. Patterns persist, and patterns repeat. The love and sense of belonging that was lacking in childhood cannot be replaced. That is extremely sad and difficult to accept, both intellectually and emotionally. Yet it is important to experience the emotion—whatever it might be—associated with recognizing that things did not turn out as you would have wished. In expressing that emotion—whether sadness, anger, rage or bewilderment—you will move from despair toward integrity. You will gain a greater acceptance of yourself. And, primarily, this journey is about *you*.

An unmet longing to belong will likely interfere with your ability to establish trusting, intimate relationships with other adults. It may also have affected your relationship with your own children. However, all is not lost. Although it might not be possible to recapture the unconditional love of a parent, it is possible to love others and to be loved by them, to have very deep and satisfactory relationships. It is still possible, at the end of life, to deepen relationships with people you love and with those who love you. That was experienced and very clearly stated by the people who participated in my study.

In reviewing parent–child relationships, many people recognize that their experience lies on a continuum between security and abandonment. The nearer the experience lies to abandonment, the greater the sense that a basic trust has been broken. When trust is broken, people feel betrayed. When a child has been betrayed by abuse or neglect, later relationships in adulthood are usually characterized by the same pattern, that is, they form bonds with adults who are likely to betray them. Eventually, they learn to avoid intimacy for fear of being hurt again.

When a sense of belonging is absent from your family of origin, there is a feeling of being ostracized, of grief. When a sense of belonging is present, there is inner peace and comfort. The longing to belong that characterizes all relationships can be met within a family of origin, with a spouse or partner, with children, and with friends. Even if there is no sense of belonging within one's family of origin or adult family, it can be developed through other relationships.

By speaking of relationships with parents, siblings, partners, children and friends, people express their need for belonging. Some of my co-researchers spoke of the pain they experienced in feeling rejected and ostracized; all valued the need for love, affection and belonging, especially at the end of life.

Through the following exercise, I invite you to explore the sense of belonging in your own life. The purpose of the exercise is to review and examine your significant relationships, beginning with your parents, your siblings and other family members. This may be of value to you in defining and understanding your own sense of belonging.

Starting with your childhood, describe your relationship with your parents. Appreciate who they were and, if they are still alive, who they are to you today. But keep in mind that this exercise is about you, not about them.

If you experience deep pain with regard to these questions, you can choose to speak to someone you trust about your feelings. If, through the course of your conversations, you are unable to finish speaking about your feelings without crying uncontrollably, you may want to seek help from a professional (counselor, psychologist, member of the clergy, etc.). If you have not cried for a long time, you may feel sad without actually crying. Just because you have not expressed an emotion does not mean it does not exist within you.

Do you remember your mother and father being warm, caring, open and responsible for you?

....
....
....
....
....
....
....
....

Do you remember them being unavailable (physically and emotionally)?

....
....
....
....
....

How did they react when you made mistakes, when you said things they didn't want to hear, when you messed up, when you were rebellious?

....
....
....
....
....
....

....

....

What emotions do you feel when you remember your childhood?

....

....

....

....

....

....

Which memories result in pleasant feelings?

....

....

....

....

....

....

Which memories result in unpleasant or painful feelings?

....

....

....

....

Could you approach your parents with questions on any topics, any emotional issues and concerns, all ideas that were important to you?

Were there unmentionable topics in your home, unmentionable activities and ideas?

Were you loved unconditionally?

What about your relationships with your siblings, aunts, uncles, grandparents?

How do you feel about the other relationships in your life (spouse, partner, friends)?

Are your relationships to those people based on trust, a sense of safety, a feeling of inclusion, or do you fear closeness, intimacy and trust even with them?

....
....
....
....
....
....
....

Have you been in long-lasting friendships and relationships, or do you have a hard time building a trusting relationship?

....
....
....
....
....
....
....
....

You might consider writing letters to some of these people, again beginning with your parents. The letters are for your benefit, to enhance your understanding. You do not need to send them; you can choose to destroy the letters or file them away as part of the legacy you leave behind. You could begin your letter by expressing gratitude for what the person gave you and then state what you think was missing in the relationship, what you wish you could have received from them. If you have become estranged from the person you are writing to, you might want to tell him or her who you have become, what is important to you, and that you have met people in your adult life who have been there for you, have understood who you are. When you have completed the letter, you may have a deeper understanding of yourself. You might also become aware of things you want to say to someone.

This is challenging, yet very important, work. You will need courage to complete this work of review and self-reflection. It is the type of courage I often witnessed in people who spoke about living with dying. They looked inward despite their fear, their desire to ignore the past and their pain. Through the process of doing this work, many of them spoke of feeling healed despite the fact that they had a terminal illness.

EIGHT

Who Am I?

Most of us live a life that is routine and familiar, at work, at home and in other activities and relationships that keep us busy. When people no longer deny death and know they are dying, their new awareness often inspires a process of life review. As an inherent part of that process, people speak their truth, recognize a longing to belong since birth and through-out their lifetime, realize who they really are, and ultimately achieve or discover a transcendence, a spirituality that extends from the core of their being to a spirit that cannot be con-tained. For some, the process may follow this sequence; for others the process happens all at once or in a different sequence, in part or as a whole. One cannot predict who will be affected by the reality, when it might hit them or how it might affect them. Through life review, we recognize patterns, successes and failures. We understand in a new way that the end of life is affected by a lifetime of relationships, activities, values and beliefs. The ending is not divorced from the begin-ning; the beginning is not separate from the end. In time, some of us wonder what happened to the dreams and aspirations we once had, in the lives we lived. Ultimately, we may feel estranged from who we really are and yearn for a life that has more meaning.

To connect with the inner self—what many call the soul—we must go on an inward journey. Many people say to themselves, "My life is going to end and I have never been me. I don't even know who 'me' is. I feel something or someone has been lost, and that someone is me. Am I living by the norms and expectations of others without recognizing my own uniqueness? Have I realized who I truly am?"

Ask yourself the question, *Who am I?* How do you define yourself?

....

....

....

....

....

....

....

....

....

....

....

You might consider beginning with your name. What is your full name? How did you get that name? What does it mean to you today? Have you ever changed your name, and why? Would you like to have a different name today? If you had chosen your own name, what would it be?

I am _____(your name).
That name was given to me because

_____

_____

_____

_____

_____

_____

_____

Are you living the life you would really like to live? If not, what is it that you need to leave behind in order to embark on your journey? Is it an old sense of self that is all too comfortable, a relationship that is detrimental to your well-being, or something that provides security for you that might need to be left behind?

_____

_____

_____

_____

_____

_____

_____

_____

Virginia Satir, a pioneer in family therapy, stated, "Many people in the world still feel moving beyond their status quo means risking death. This attitude toward change can be one of the greatest hindrances to personal growth and effective therapy. In this frame of mind, people sometimes prefer a familiar dysfunction to an unknown improvement or comfort." For many, the diagnosis of a terminal illness or the experience of that illness serves as a catalyst for a personal awakening. It ends the routine and the indifference. People are no longer paralyzed by the fear that moving beyond their status quo means risking death. They know that death is inevitable, and therefore experience a new freedom to live authentically.

Because they know that they cannot escape death, they embrace life—their own life. The prescription of how to live given by family, culture, profession, religion or friends loses its grasp. Perhaps, in this way, knowing that you have a terminal illness is of value. Knowing that dying is part of living might also be experienced as meaningful by those of us who do not have a diagnosis of a terminal illness. What about those who are living with a chronic illness? Those who are aging? When do I begin asking the same questions as people who know they have a terminal illness are asking? What am I waiting for? What can I (each of us) learn about living from those who know they are dying? What might I come to know about myself if I confronted my own mortality? Would that change how I live? Would that change any of my relationships?

Peggy was a 63-year-old woman dying of lung cancer. Thirty years earlier, Peggy had had breast cancer. Peggy spoke of being what the world of her childhood wanted her to be. She described her ancestors. "They're old families. On my French-Canadian side we're sort of settlers in Canada, way back. On the other side, my father was a lord, and there's a lot of history there too. My girls are very proud of it. They don't capitalize on it or anything, but family history has been very much a part of their upbringing and who I am. I was an only child. Although I didn't realize it at the time, it probably was a very lonely life."

Following her diagnosis of breast cancer, Peggy began asking the question, *Who am I?*

> I think the big thing is that I was an only child. I was a thing owned by my parents. I was dressed up and brought up to say "good evening" during the cocktail hour. There was a lack of connection because I was brought up by nannies and governesses. For that reason, I loved boarding school. (As a mother, I went in the

other direction: I didn't want a nanny and practically never used a babysitter.)

My sense of self was not to be found. I couldn't satisfy my parents. If I got an A, why didn't I get an A-plus? My mother was an alcoholic, and everybody around her was an alcoholic.

The pattern of her family of origin was repeated. She married a man who, like her father, disregarded her efforts. Peggy became an alcoholic. "My husband was very, very British. You know what it's like: He walks in the door, the baby's crying. 'Can't you shut it up?' The kids ended up having the same upbringing I had. The kids were seen and not heard. My life changed once I started to accept that I was an alcoholic. I looked around and saw hundreds of people around me who enjoyed life." At this point, she had to confront the isolation she felt in her family of origin, which seemed to be in sharp contrast to the people around her who were enjoying life. She also had to confront the fact that she had been living for the approval of others.

Peggy realized that she had been using alcohol to drown her pain and that even though she had stopped drinking, she was still an alcoholic. Before that realization, she wanted to avoid pain at any cost, to be distracted from the work of looking in the mirror to see who she really was.

According to Dr. Walter Toman, author of *Family Constellation*, as a female only child, there might be a tendency to "structure her life around older people, people in authority and superiors; to obtain their approval and hopefully their preferential treatment." Peggy recognized that pattern in her own relationship with her father: "My sense of self was not to be found. I just couldn't please him." Peggy had a sense of not being good enough. On one level, she was determined to do better next time, in the hope of pleasing her father. On another level, she came to believe that there was something wrong with her unless she was perfect. (In most cases like this, the child strives for perfection). Peggy believed that she was valued for her performance rather than for who she was as a person. She learned to live according to expectations, ignoring her own sense of self, ignoring her own limitations. She would continue to strive for perfection and parental approval, always falling short, always reminded that she was failing. At times she might have believed that she was a failure as a person. She discounted her own feelings, gradually losing her identity; like her mother, she would come to numb her pain with alcohol.

An important question for each of us is: *Am I living my life for the approval of others?* If so, how? What about the life I really want to live? Am I able to live a life that beckons me and intimidates me at the same time? How do I pursue it?

....

....

....

....

....

....

....

The pattern recurred in Peggy's relationship with her husband, for she recognized in it the same demand for perfection.

A child in a situation like this would internalize the message that there was something wrong with her. This usually results in a sense of shame, described by John Bradshaw, a well-known family therapist, as "toxic shame."

Shame is a painful feeling of humiliation or distress caused by the consciousness of wrong or foolish behavior. As such, shame serves a purpose in our relationships with one another and in society as a whole. Who I am and what I do are separate entities. If I feel shame for what I do, I can correct the behavior; if I feel shame for who I am because I have been led to believe that I am flawed, that there is something inherently wrong with me, my sense of self suffers. That means I, and perhaps my family, would be better off if that part of me did not exist, if that part of me died. This is the shame Bradshaw defines as toxic shame, or

> the shame that binds you, [which] is experienced as the all-pervasive sense that I am flawed and defective as a human being. Toxic shame is no longer an emotion that signals our limits, it is a state of being, a core identity. Toxic shame gives you a sense of worthlessness, a sense of failing and falling short as a human being. Toxic shame is a rupture of the self with the self.

In the context of that definition, Bradshaw speaks of developing a false self from the pain of being unacceptable as one's true self. The false self is found in the superachieving perfectionist just as often as it is in the addict in the alley. "[T]he most paradoxical aspect of neurotic [i.e., toxic] shame is that it is the core motivator of the superachieved and the underachieved, the Star and the Scapegoat, the Righteous and the wretched, the powerful and the pathetic." Think of "toxic" as synonymous with "poison." Poison damages, injures and destroys. Shame that damages, injures or destroys who we are, could certainly be regarded as poisonous or toxic.

Peggy spoke about her mother: "My mother had some very good qualities; she was a very clever lady. But she had an unhappy upbringing."

You may wonder about relationships with family members or other people who expect you to be something you feel that is not true to your character, your personality, your sense of self. You may realize for the first time that your relationship with your family of origin is not, or was not, what you wanted it to be. You may also recognize a pattern in your relationships beginning in childhood and adolescence. This might result in emotional pain or discomfort.

Peggy assumed responsibility for her own life. By seeking help through counseling and by acknowledging that Alcoholics Anonymous had become her lifeline, Peggy began to change the course of her family history. She stepped into and through her pain. She understood the source of her toxic shame. She became more aware of her shadow self; that is, she became conscious of the part of herself she had been unaware of up to that point in her life, and so became more wholly who she was.

Peggy wanted to look at the whole picture of who she was, for only then could she truly begin to like herself. She also realized that she mattered to some people. "So that sense of no self-worth is leaving. I am very grateful I can see it that way, and I'm hoping it comes through with those close to me. I think it will." Peggy spoke of her sense of self: "You know, I guess it has changed. I think that I can face death liking myself now. I think that's the big difference. Facing death has shown me that I've got the inner strength. I'd say that's the essence of it." A hope-filled essence indeed!

In becoming true to yourself, a new person emerges, one who may not be recognized by others. Wearing a mask is how we present ourselves to others (the perfect mother/father, the wise teacher, the compassionate doctor, the successful business person, etc.). The clothes we wear, the words we speak, how we say them, and our actions, tell others about who we are. Carl Jung spoke of this mask as being the "persona," the Greek word for mask. We can choose to hide features of who we are—our weaknesses, for example—if we do not want others to see them. Hiding weaknesses reduces our vulnerability. In that way, the mask provides a protective covering. It also means that some features of who we are do not come to light. In essence, they are what Jung described as our "shadow." Often, these are qualities we are ashamed of having. The shadow also includes "aspects of ourselves that might yet be lived out, our unlived life—talents and abilities that have long been buried or never been conscious." Perhaps another term we could use to define or describe our shadow is our "wild side"—the part of us that is unknown, untamed, unrecognized.

Wearing a mask is our attempt to compromise between our real identity and the expectations of others; it is a compromise between who we are and what we are willing to reveal. It helps us interact with other people. Sometimes people take their mask so seriously that they believe it truly reflects who they are. They forget about or ignore their shadow, their wild side. It is only when people distinguish between their mask— that is, the person they appear to be—and their real identity, that the process of answering the question, *Who am I?* really begins. This results in a decreased identification with the mask and an increased assimilation of the shadow. You can stop playing games and be honest and truthful with yourself and others.

We adopt the stance, the culture, the habits, the perspective of the world around us—the world of our families, communities, institutions, workplaces and professions. What is it in us that results in an awakening to our true self?

Frederick Buechner, a theologian, describes the situation:

> [T]he world sets in to making us into what the world would like us to be, and because we have to survive after all, we try to make ourselves into something that we hope the world will like better than it apparently did the selves we originally were. That is the story of all our lives, needless to say, and in the process of living out that story, the original, shimmering self gets buried so deep that most of us end up hardly living out of it at all. Instead we live out all the other selves which we are constantly putting on and taking off like coats and hats against the world's weather.

James Hollis also describes this process:

> [W]hatever reality may be, it will to some extent be shaped by the lens through which we see it. When we are born we are handed multiple lenses: genetic inheritance, gender, a specific culture and the variables of our family environment, all of which constitute our sense of reality. Looking back later we have to admit that we have perhaps lived less from our true nature than from the

vision of reality ordained by the lenses we used. Although each person is born with multiple lenses, she also makes choices to become the person she is.

The process of "waking up to oneself"—that is, the process of individuation—beckons everyone at some point in life. As a process, it is never complete and becomes more of a quest than a goal. For some it may begin in adolescence, for others it is manifest through the emotional despair of a mid-life crisis, some catastrophic event, or difficult circumstances (divorce or threat of separation, financial difficulties, problems at work, illness, or the death of a family member or friend). And if it has not occurred before learning that one has a terminal illness, the longing to know and understand one's self—to answer the question *Who am I?*—often emerges from the experience of living with a terminal illness.

To know who we are as adults, we must understand who we were as children, in the context of our family of origin. This is strengthened by knowing the context of our family history through past generations. For in understanding the context of our family of origin, we begin to understand and appreciate "who the world wanted us to be."

A feature of knowing one has a terminal illness is visiting or revisiting one's place in—one's relationship to—the family of origin. Even for someone who has already done this, the need recurs at the end of life. It can happen in the context of an adult relationship with one's family, whether that's the family of origin or of choice. It pertains to one's understanding of self. With the understanding comes a sense of peace and, for some, a sense of meaning. This process seems to mark the experience of living with a terminal illness. One's experience of childhood is a reality throughout life, whether that person remains in the family community or moves far away. Understanding that context is part of answering the *Who am I?* question.

I invite you to draw another timeline or add to one of the time-lines you have already drawn. Draw the timeline. As you did previously, place an X one centimeter to the left of the word Death, and add a dotted line beyond the word Death. In addi-tion, draw a dotted line that precedes the word Birth.

- - - - - - *Birth*————————————————X—*Death* - - - - - -

Again, write your name below the X. What do you feel as you write your name this time?

Many of the questions that follow pertain to the time prior to your birth; that is, the time marked by the dotted line preced-ing the word Birth on the time line. Those features of your life also contributed to who you are today. What were the circum-stances surrounding your birth? What was your family like at the time? How many others were in the family? Were you born or adopted into the family? Perhaps you were a foster child. Were you welcomed? Were you celebrated? How was the fam-ily system affected by your birth?

....
....
....
....
....
....
....
....
....

What are some of the family patterns that have occurred from generation to generation? How many generations are known by you or by other family members?

....
....
....
....

How would your father describe his relationship to each of his parents?

....
....
....
....
....
....

What is known about your paternal grandparents' relationships to each of their parents?

....
....
....
....
....
....

Similarly, how would your mother describe her relationship to each of her parents?

....
....
....
....
....
....

What is known about your maternal grandparents' relationships to each of their parents?

....
....
....
....
....
....

Was there illness (physical or mental) in their families, was there a history of addiction, were there family traits that were passed on from generation to generation that affected the family, were there secrets that created taboos in the family? Did any of your family serve in a war? Who, and how many generations ago? How did that family history affect your childhood, adulthood, and/or present situation? How is the relationship with my children similar to the relationship I had with my parents? Is there anything I would like to do or say in order to change the pattern?

_____

_____

_____

_____

_____

_____

_____

_____

_____

_____

For Brent, the stimulus to ask the question *Who am I?* arose from his close encounter with death. His process of awakening began with a near-death experience:

> I'm really taking control of my life and that's because, in coming so close to death, you realize that if you don't take control no one will do it for you. You have to separate from your family to become a person. I realized

when I was dying that I was going to die alone, that no one was coming with me; I was going alone. Then I realized that each person's journey is truly one of aloneness and that whatever happens in your life, it's only you, it's always going to be only you.

For Brent, asking *Who am I?* was linked to speaking his truth and hearing the truth of others.

If you can't be bothered to tell me the truth, don't tell me anything, because there's nothing else but the truth. This is who I am, take it or leave it. I don't put on airs. I used to think it was really important what clothes you wore. All the things that used to matter so much, they don't matter any more.

By looking inward, he re-experienced the pain of his childhood.

My childhood was painful. You know we were adopted children. We were treated poorly by our parents, two people who were very religious. They must have thought that they were doing their duty, that they were giving some poor children a good home. I do believe that's what they honestly felt. They believed they were doing the right thing, but what they actually did, and I think they forget this, is they took the lives of four children and potentially ruined them.

That was a difficult statement for Brent to make. He could appreciate that his parents had done their best. At the same time, he realized that his life was about *him,* not about his parents doing their best. He had to learn to separate from his family in order to learn to be an individual. That was as true for his parents as it was for him. With regard to family expectations, he said, *"I don't want to play that game any more. I want to live in the truth. And whether they want to deal with it or not is irrelevant at this point."*

Everyone needs to separate from his family of origin to become his own person. For Brent, that meant being confronted by his own mortality and going through a process of self-reflection, which helped him become aware of his own uniqueness.

Imagine for a moment that you have been informed that you have a terminal illness, a frightening thought, perhaps. If that meant you had six months or even a year of life left, how would you live it? What would you do differently? How would that information affect your relationships, decisions, activities?

When you confront your own mortality, the person other people expect you to be falls away, and a new self is born—or rather, your original self surfaces. In Brent's words,

> And that's what I think makes us lucky. When you come close to death, all that crap just flies off of you; it just sort of comes off you like layers of skin. All of a sudden, you're starting from scratch, like when you were born. And all of those messages that you were taught, all of the negative stuff is replaced with positive things, loving things, caring things, things that make you a better, happier person. I believe in myself now. I never had that before. And I am not afraid of being who I am.

Brent spoke about his wishes for his last days.

> If the family or friends can't or don't want to deal with these issues, then at least you face up to that. Everybody can pretend they're getting along, but I don't want to pretend. That doesn't get you anywhere.

For Brent, that meant stating that his father could not bear to be at his bedside as he died. His father could not say that he loved his son. Brent could no longer pretend that there was a loving relationship between them. He wanted to move beyond the shame he felt. For him,

> Resolution is simply the truth—good, bad, or indifferent. It's the truth, and that's all that seems to matter when you're at that point. You know where you're going, and you feel good about where you're going.

You just don't want to bring this negative stuff along with you.

He realized he would never have his father's love. To come to that understanding and to say it aloud was, for Brent, a painful process. In experiencing such pain, Brent integrated the truth into his reality. He not only spoke the truth; he accepted it into his sense of himself. He moved through the despair experienced in that truth, toward integrity.

Resolution lay in understanding and speaking the truth. Brent believed that without resolution within himself, he would exist in a state of turmoil right up to the moment of his death.

> Dying bottled up would be horrible. I can only imagine
> it's like going to hell. I think that would be awful because
> you'd carry that around with you for all eternity. And if
> there is such a thing as reincarnation, you would come
> back with that turmoil within you. It has to be resolved
> in this lifetime, I believe.

Here are two important things to remember with regard to your childhood and your family of origin. First, each pregnancy changes the family, in that it will either result in a miscarriage, which is a death, or a birth, which marks the addition of a new family member. Your parents and, to some extent, your siblings, will be affected by your birth. That is also true for you as subsequent births and deaths occur in the family. Second, your memory is your story and your truth. Your family members will have experienced the same events differently and will likely have different memories. Your experience and understanding of events is legitimate; the same holds true for other family members.

When a child is not accepted for who she is by her parents, she begins to perform for acceptance. That means she is unable to grow into her uniqueness, but instead becomes the product of the expectations of the home and community. Dr. Murray Bowen, a psychiatrist who produced a new theory of human behavior—the family systems theory—describes the need to differentiate. He uses the formation of the embryo in his explanation. Groups of cells that are identical in the beginning of a developing fetus eventually differentiate in order to form the different organs of the body. While that happens on a physical basis, the psychological development of the child is similar, in that the child grows into a being that is different from the parents.

The more children are accepted for who they are, the greater their ability to differentiate, to cope with the demands of life and reach their goals. All children learn who they are through the people around them. For most children, and as stated in the previous chapter, that begins with their parents, who serve as a mirror and an echo for the child. That message is transmitted primarily by action and attitude; even the infant receives the message in the pre-verbal years. Children who are loved unconditionally learn that they are inherently lovable and acceptable. Parents who have misgivings about themselves or have poor self-esteem will project that message onto the child. The child will see and experience that attitude, interpreting it to mean that it arises from how the parent feels about her. For the child, looking into the parent's face is like looking in a mirror, hearing the parent's voice is like hearing an echo. The child has no reason to doubt the message the parent is giving. That is why it is particularly important that in the first years of a child's life she be taken seriously, that she be accepted for who she is. What does that mean specifically?

Alice Miller, the author of *The Drama of the Gifted Child*, describes the dynamics of effective mirroring, an essential feature of parenting. To begin with, the parent knows that the child is a separate being and loves him as a separate being. When the child is aggressive or expresses anger, the parent is not threatened but is able to respond to the child's behavior. As an example, consider the young child who has a temper tantrum in a grocery store. You might have seen parents threaten the child by telling the child that they will leave the child in the store—a strong statement of abandonment. Another common response is for the parent to express rage and anger to the same degree as the child is expressing rage and anger. Neither the abandonment statement nor the rage will serve as a mirror of security and love. A parent who is self-confident, not threatened, would remove the child from the public space in a gentle yet firm manner. Once the two are outside the store, the parent might hold the child very securely, speaking calmly to the child. This would eventually eliminate the child's own fear about the emotion. He would learn that anger is an acceptable emotion, that it can be expressed, and that the parent will not withhold love from him during the temper tantrum.

Similarly, a child may be allowed to express ordinary impulses—jealousy, rage, sexuality, defiance—because the parents have not disowned these feelings in themselves. The child can be dependent as a foundation to independence, the child can leave or approach the parents as necessary, confident that the parents will be available when the child needs them. His natural striving for autonomy is not seen as a threat by the parents. Such children can develop their own needs at their own developmental pace. Parents live their lives and allow children to live theirs. Until we understand how the influence of childhood affected who we are as adults, our understanding of who we are as adults will be limited. We may be children who grow old, or grow older without growing up, rather than children who become adults and take their place in the world.

In speaking of her family of origin as well as her adult family, Peggy was addressing who she was. Knowing and understanding the relationships in her family of origin enabled her to understand herself more fully and clearly. Although this process had started several years prior to her diagnosis, the issues surfaced again as she reviewed her life. Peggy seemed to appreciate that her real self grew out of a complex interaction of her genetic composition (nature), the experience of being a product of her family of origin (nurture), and her own choices.

The wounds of the first generation hurt the second, the wounds of the second hurt the third, and so on, until someone like Peggy suffers enough to break the chain. Peggy's father expected her to be perfect, most likely because that was expected of him as a child. Peggy's mother was an alcoholic. Peggy followed the script of her childhood—being a perfectionist, trying to meet all the expectations of her parents, failing to acknowledge, feel, or express her pain—into adulthood, where she continued to live by the same script. But she suffered enough psychologically that she was prepared to break the chain by changing her behavior and pattern of relationships. This is summarized by James Hollis:

Fate provides the initial wounding and the flawed parenting of each subsequent generation, and yet all are
responsible for the lives they have chosen—as we too are
responsible for our choices and their consequences.

This was apparent in Peggy's life: for a time she followed a
course similar to her mother's. However, the difference
between the two women was in Peggy's choice to live a different life, to alter the course of her family history such that her
children would benefit from living with a mother who had
confronted and addressed the issues of being an alcoholic.

There is value in asking, how might I be living or carrying
within me the unlived life of my parent? What is that life?
Where am I in exactly the same position as my parent in that
regard?

_____

_____

_____

_____

_____

_____

There is benefit in telling your story to at least one other person, especially if you have experienced toxic shame in your
life. Choose the listener carefully. You must feel completely
safe; whatever you say must be accepted without judgment. It
would be wise to select somebody who has already proven to
be able to listen to you—not just hear you—but to *listen* to

you. The person you choose must realize that this is about you, not about them. This is *your* story. It is not the time for them to begin to tell you about their childhood, their story, their toxic shame, their psychological wounds.

Speak to that person about toxic shame, looking into the listener's eyes. This will be difficult, for we avoid eye contact when we feel ashamed of what we have done or if we feel shame in who we are. The listener might ask questions for clarification. After you finish your story, ask your listener what they understand about your experience and what they were feeling as you spoke.

The experience of learning about a terminal illness can propel someone into a search for the true self, a search for healing, for the courage to care for psychological wounds. It is the only way to live life to the fullest until one dies. One discards what's imitation and embraces what's real. This is a continuous process, which seems to move people from depression toward hope, through anxiety toward peace, and from despair toward integrity.

In being confronted by death, Brent realized who he was. He also realized that to be truly alive it was important to be real—to be himself—regardless of his remaining time on earth.

> When you're dying, you're stripped of everything that's important to society—money, image—so all you have left is that honesty. It takes so much energy to pretend when you can use that energy for other things. Part of me died in that hospital, a part of me died, the part that was bitter, angry, resentful, hateful and spiteful, died. Now there's a new person.

After suffering through the anger he'd lived with all his life, Brent began to experience a new compassion and ability to listen to others. When a nurse helped him after a bout of incontinence, he said,

> If I was still worried about what people thought about me, I think I wouldn't have noticed her care or listened to what she was saying, because I would've been so concerned about being dirty and the humiliation of needing her to clean me. But she did it with such dignity and made me feel like there was nothing wrong.

In dying, many people find their true self. Brent experienced a new level of perception.

> You do wake up. It's like a revelation of some sort. All of a sudden, all these things that were hidden are now front and centre. There's no hiding from them any more. I belong to me now, and that's how I think I've survived.

To die outside one's truth is to die wounded, whereas to understand one's truth and accept it is to die healed—not cured, but healed. To heal is always possible, even when cure is impossible. As Brent says,

> Don't lie to yourself, because that only makes it more difficult to fight the physical disease. By telling yourself the truth, you allow yourself to heal. You're not so busy trying to play games, and so your mind has more time to work on your body. The mind and body really do work together. If your mind is so busy trying to keep you from

thinking about the truth, your body is going to be neg-
lected; it's not going to get that chance it needs to heal.
It's funny how people will just deny it 'til they die.

Both Peggy and Brent looked inward. They had been living
under the masks that suited the world around them. Both
experienced toxic shame because their parents were unable to
accept them as they were. In stepping into their true selves,
each of them had to "leave home." They worked to understand who they had been during their childhood years, how
they had lived up to the expectations of their families, and how
they had thereby denied the expression and development of
who they were as individuals. Peggy suffered through an addiction to alcohol before she realized that she did not need to
measure up to the expectations of anyone else, that she had
her own worth—her self-worth. Brent was able to articulate
that his father and sisters could not accept who he was as a
gay male.

   Erik Erikson developed a theory of the life cycle that
divided life into eight stages. He presented the cycle such that
each stage could be understood in the context of the laws of
individual development and social organization. An understanding of the eighth stage—despair versus integrity—
enhances one's understanding when learning about a terminal illness.

   Erikson defines despair as a "feeling that the time is
short, too short for the attempt to start another life and to try
out alternate roads to integrity." Following the work of
Erikson, Judith Herman, a psychiatrist at Harvard Medical
School and director of training for the Victims of Violence
Program at Cambridge Hospital, defines integrity as "the

capacity to affirm the value of life in the face of death, to be reconciled with the finite limits of one's own life and the tragic limitations of the human condition, and to accept these realities without despair."

Peggy and Brent lived with integrity. They were willing to look at themselves, warts and all. They were prepared to acknowledge the price they had paid by living in dishonesty and pain from wounds that were generations deep. In so doing, they experienced despair. Despair might include anxiety and depression, experiences that are generally seen as threats to one's sense of well-being, particularly at the end of life. But they knew that what leads to despair, no matter how painful, can also lead to enhanced self-awareness and meaning.

It is meaning that delivers people from despair to integrity. To find meaning, we must be willing to embark on a journey— an encounter with the past, with the core of one's being.

This is no different for those with a terminal illness or those who are not ready to confront mortality. For many people who know they have a terminal illness, the knowledge in itself provides the impetus and the courage to go places where they would rather not go. Therein lies the irony. For one person, knowing you have a terminal illness can result in the belief that the real opportunities of life have passed; for another it is an indication that life has just begun.

I have been telling you about others, how they made and found meaning in their lives. But perhaps this is an opportunity for *you* to begin thinking about your life and who you are. The following is a self-reflective exercise that you can do right now to begin the process. It might lead to a fuller understanding of who you are. In doing this exercise, you might discover that there is more to be explored, that is, beyond the questions

I pose. If that's the case, I recommend you contact a professional counselor or therapist. By working with one, you can more fully complete the work you have yet to do.

Find a space where you will not be interrupted. Make yourself comfortable. Sit quietly for a period, thinking about who you were as a child.

Imagine that you are seven years old. Draw or imagine a triangle (adapted from Birren and Deutchman, "Metaphors and Triangulation of the Self"). Each point on the triangle has a label: your ideal self (how you would like to be), your social image self (how others see you), and your real self (how you see yourself). For each of these selves choose something that most accurately describes you at that age. If you like, choose an animal, a character from literature, or a piece of music. Remembering your favorite activities, friends, stories, music and games might help you. How did you relate to your parents and your siblings at that time?

Describe in thought or in writing how you understand yourself to be each of those labels, each of those points on the triangle. Repeat the exercise, remembering yourself at seven-year intervals until you get to your present age (i.e., as a fourteen-year-old adolescent, a twenty-one-year-old young adult, and so on). Make certain to do the exercise at your present age. As you look at the collage of who you were and who you have become, in which picture is the ideal self, the social image self, and the real self most similar?

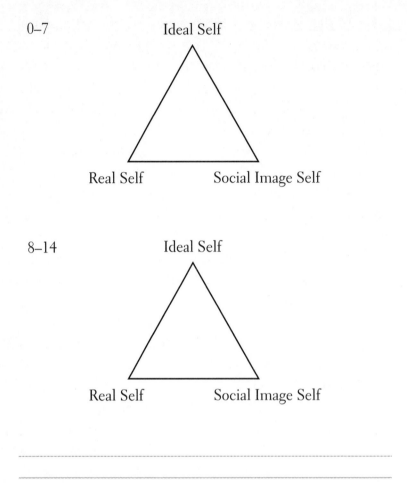

0–7

Ideal Self

Real Self   Social Image Self

8–14

Ideal Self

Real Self   Social Image Self

....

....

....

....

....

....

....

....

....

....

....

....

As you do all or part of this exercise, I trust that you will gain some insight into who you are, how you believe others might see you, and how or who you would like to be. You might ask a close friend or family member to respond to your sense of self. You may also choose to spend some time thinking and reflecting on how you understand your self, or you might ask a professional counselor to guide you through a process of gaining new insights and understanding.

NINE

Experiencing Spirituality at the End of Life

> My cup of joy is full to overflowing and that which over-flows is also full; for as that which is physical within me gets weaker, that which is spiritual gets ever stronger.
>
> —Peggy

A spiritual journey brings our whole being into question. As we become quiet to listen to the voice of our hearts, we begin to hear, to see, to experience, and to know and understand who we really are. Spirituality has to do with silence. It also has to do with a focus on being awake, listening and paying attention.

Get into a comfortable sitting position, close your eyes, take a few slow, deep breaths as you imagine yourself to be a fast-flowing river. Winding your way across the land, you pick up some of whatever covers the banks of the river. Therefore the water is murky and full of debris. Over time and over distance the river slows, and the contents settle to the bottom of the river. Eventually, the water is no longer fast-flowing, it is still; it is no longer filled with debris. The river has become a deep pool of pure, crystal-clear water. You are that pool of water. How do you feel? What do you see? What color is the water? Is it warm or cold? As you sit quietly, what message emerges from the stillness, from the depth of that pool, and through the clarity of the water?[1] In silence and in stillness we are able to listen and hear an inner voice, a voice of authenticity. Questions surface. New ideas come into view, some very familiar, some very foreign. And in time, an understanding of who we are begins to emerge.

What did you feel, what were you aware of inside yourself as you listened? What questions and/or ideas emerged?

....

....

....

....

....

....

Only people with a terminal illness know what it means to live with a terminal illness. What do they say about that experience? They speak about themselves, their relationships (past and present) with others, their sense of transcendence. That was the experience of of Peggy and Brent. Peggy spoke of accepting herself; Brent spoke of wholeness. Peggy grew to accept herself over a seven-year period, coming to appreciate that the spiritual dimension within her was growing through

---

1. Adapted from a visualization exercise led by Dr. Micheal Kearney, XIth International Congress on Care of the Terminally Ill, Montreal, Quebec, 1996.

her honesty, her pain, and with time. Brent realized his sense of wholeness through his near-death experience, and then went through a process of accepting who he was. He moved from a place of self-loathing to a place of feeling healed and whole. He felt that in his near-death experience he had been in the presence of a Higher Power (the term Higher Power will be used through this chapter as reference to a Spiritual Being/Essence, that which is greater than humanness. The term is chosen with respect for the people who participated in the research project) that loved him unconditionally, and therefore he was able to begin to love himself unconditionally as well.

What might people who are living with a terminal illness say about spirituality? How does one begin to speak or write about spirituality when much about spirituality has to do with mystery? Inherent in the concept of Mystery is that which cannot be named nor defined. What, then, are the words that describe the experience? How does one avoid cliché? How does one write about something so intangible, yet so real? And how does one avoid definition, as definition diminishes mystery, the very essence we are working to understand?

People who know they have a terminal illness, who know they are dying, speak about the spiritual. Their spiritual journey is not about escaping from their lives, their reality, their past, their troubles or their pain. Their conversations about the spiritual seem not to have the boundaries and limitations of religion. Many of their conversations have nothing to do with commitment to a particular religion. In fact, the conversations are primarily about who they are, and not so much about the dogma or ideals of a religious perspective. They speak about the reality or the desire for a deep sense of connection to themselves, to others, and to something greater (a Higher Power, Nature, Goddess, God, Buddha, the Creator, Allah, Christ, etc.) than themselves. To them, the name is not as important as the sense, the essence, the reality of something beyond our humanness. Their description of the spiritual includes concepts such as truth, choice, Nature, love, forgiveness, resolution, self-acceptance, gratitude and inner strength. It has to do with the past, the present and the future; it also has to do with the good, the bad and the ugly in their lives, that is, spirituality has to do with wholeness.

Before you read any further I invite you to participate in one more timeline or life-line exercise. As before, on a sheet of unlined paper, draw a horizontal, diagonal or vertical line. On the left side of the line write the word Birth, and on the right side of the line write the word Death. Add a dotted line about 3 centimeters long preceding the word Birth and another 3-centimeter line following the word Death.

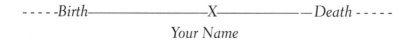

- - - - -Birth———————X—————— Death - - - - -
Your Name

Again, think of this line as representing your lifetime. As you did the first time, place an X on the line to indicate where you believe you are at present. That is, if you believe that you have lived half of your life, place the X midway between Birth and Death. If you believe that you have lived two-thirds of your life, place the X two-thirds of the way along the line. Once you have placed the X on the line, write your name below the X. And as I suggested for previous exercises, similar to this one, take note of your feelings.

Think back over your lifetime.

Name six things that you have done that brought goodness to someone else. Who was the person? What were the circumstances? How did the other person respond? What effect did it have on you at the time?

1. _____

_____

_____

2. _____

_____

_____

3. _____

_____

_____

4. _____

_____

_____

5. _____

_____

_____

6. _____

_____

_____

What do you feel as you remember this goodness in your life?

_____

_____

_____

_____

_____

Name six things that you have done that give you meaning.

1. ....
....

2. ....
....

3. ....
....

4. ....
....

5. ....
....

6. ....
....

What do you feel as you remember the meaning in your life?

....
....
....
....
....
....

Name six features of your life you are thankful for.

1. ....

2. ....

3. ....

4. ....

5. ....

6. ....

What do you feel as you focus on gratitude in your life?

....

....

....

....

....

....

....

....

Name three to six values that have been important to you through your lifetime. How did you adopt these values as being important? Are they important to you today? How do they affect your life?

1. ....
....

2. ....
....

3. ....
....

4. ....
....

5. ....
....

6. ....
....

What does spirituality mean to you?

....
....
....
....
....
....
....

Look forward over the next days, weeks, months and years—what gives you hope? Where do you find peace and how will you exercise and strengthen your spiritual self?

1. ....

....

2. ....

....

3. ....

....

4. ....

....

5. ....

....

6. ....

....

The spiritual experience of the people who participated in the study was an experience of profound love and acceptance. In that context, people were seeking to live in truth and forgiveness, thereby living with a deep understanding of wholeness and healing. For some people, learning that they had a terminal illness was a gift, a gift of time to pay close attention to who they really were, to discover a deep sense of spirituality, to grow in a sense of self-acceptance and love, such that fear of death was diminished or eliminated. They experienced a greater connectedness to others and found deeper meaning in relationships.

The experience for them was very personal and private. Strength, love and integrity resulted in a wholeness they had not previously experienced. That was strongly felt in nature, from the smallest bird, through the eyes of a doe, embracing a tree, or looking to the mountains. In nature people saw birth and the magnitude of life. They also bore witness to the reality of dying and death. In these experiences they felt a wholeness and a oneness with nature, which included an extension of the self, beyond the self, to the Higher Power. In that context, they experienced joy and purpose, and lost all fear of death.

What role does nature have in your life, especially as it pertains to the spiritual dimension of your life? Do you remember a time or a place where you were particularly aware of being part of a greater universe? (You may have considered this in the chapter on life review.)

How did the people who knew they were dying get to a place of joy and purpose without the fear of death? All of them had confronted or were confronting their own mortality. That meant making sense of who they were in the context of the lives they had lived, with the hope that in looking back they might find meaning, purpose, and perhaps some direction for the time and energy that was still remaining. It was "a long and difficult process of reclaiming emotions, of bringing awareness and understanding to patterns of relationship, of learning how to feel feelings, and to deal with the powerful forces of human connection." Looking at every area of their lives—that is, paying attention—required courage, commitment and determination. It was an active process.

Jack Kornfield, a clinical psychologist trained as a Buddhist monk, states that:

> wise spiritual practice requires that we actively address the pain and conflict in our life in order to come to inner integration and harmony . . . Many people first come to spiritual practice hoping to skip over their sorrows and wounds, the difficult areas of their lives. They hope to rise above them and enter a spiritual realm full of divine grace, free from all conflict. Some spiritual practices actually do encourage this and teach ways of accomplishing this through intense concentration and ardor that bring about states of rapture and peace. Some powerful yogic practices can transform the mind. While such practices have their value, an inevitable disappointment occurs when they end, for as soon as practitioners relax in their discipline, they again encounter all the unfinished business of the body and heart that they had hoped to leave behind . . . True maturation on the spiritual path requires that we discover that depth of our wounds: our grief from the past, unfulfilled longing, the sorrow that we have stored up during the course of our lives."

What are the manifestations of a spiritual practice such as this? How does such a practice translate into the affairs and events of one's everyday life? The stories of Peggy and Brent begin to answer those questions. It is my hope that their stories might be an inspiration and a guide to others who are on a similar crossing. You have met both of them in previous chapters.

Peggy's Story

Peggy, a 63-year-old woman, had a deep desire to know and understand herself. She also had cancer. Peggy wanted to be involved in all decisions regarding her care for as long as possible. She was alert and oriented until the last day of her life. She was able to communicate clearly about her physical, psychological and spiritual experience throughout the course of her illness.

Throughout the last years of her life, Peggy asked some difficult questions. She was prepared to look at her real life situation, her relationship with herself, with her husband and with her adult children. What was her family of origin like? What were the pains she endured because she was born into a particular family? What would someone need to know about her family of origin to understand who she was?

Peggy believed that she was valued for her performance rather than for who she was as a person. She learned to live according to expectations, ignoring her own sense of self, ignoring her own limitations. She would continue to strive for perfection and parental approval, always falling short, always reminded that she was failing to meet their expectations. At times she believed that she was a failure as a person. She discounted her own feelings, thereby gradually losing her identity. All that had been pushed away in her thoughts and in her feelings, in her mind and in her heart for decades was necessarily brought to light in being honest about herself. Honesty was a very painful yet essential ingredient of her spiritual journey, as is the case for many people who embark on such a journey.

In order to come to a new understanding of who she was, Peggy needed to review her life again and again. What was the source of her pain, where was her pain coming from? How was it that she was living her adult life in a way that was similar to how she had survived her childhood?

Peggy wanted to look at the "whole picture" of who she was, for only then could she truly begin to know and like herself. She also realized that she mattered to some people. "So that sense of no self-worth is leaving. I am very grateful I can see it that way, and I'm hoping it comes through with those close to me. I think it will." Peggy spoke of her sense of self: "You know, I guess it has changed. I think that I can face death liking myself now. I think that's the big difference. Facing death has shown me that I've got the inner strength. I'd say that's the essence of it."

The dominant theme, for Peggy, as it pertained to the spiritual was that her sense of the spiritual was her greatest resource and a tremendous source of strength and comfort for her. It was something greater than herself, for herself, in the context of which she was able to accept herself, to laugh, to love and to enjoy life.

I was from the structured religious home, I was brought up a Roman Catholic and sent to Church, then I converted to become an Anglican. The children were baptized Anglican. It was the thing to do. I have no deep beliefs. I knew there was something but I didn't stop to take time to think of it. So it wasn't really until I got into AA and started to first of all accept that I was an alcoholic. I think this is where I really learnt spirituality.

Spirituality includes a belief in a Higher Power, a Power greater than myself. I happen to be fond of nature, I can get by, just looking outside. Spirituality isn't any one thing. It comes from inside for me and when I find I'm in a very bad space and discontent and everything, I know I have to go back to basics and think of spirituality. Then I can ground myself again.

So this is the first time I'm having to adjust to knowing that I'm not going to get better. I'm finding that quite difficult, or not difficult, but I'm not used to a defeatist mindset and the spirituality is what's pulling me through. As I mentioned to you, I'm in Alcoholics Anonymous and involved quite deeply and it's done a lot for me. One of our things is "let go and let God." I've used that. I have to use the word trust in turning myself over and praying for help for my children . . . I'm acknowledging my spirituality more then I ever have.

The term "let go and let God" is a slogan which is part of Alcoholics Anonymous, a term which may seem incredibly simplistic or it may be seen to represent the core of one's spiritual being. It has been described as easy to say and difficult to follow. Peggy didn't explain the meaning of the term. In his book

Telling Secrets, Frederick Buechner explains the meaning of the slogan. When Buechner was a young boy, his father committed suicide. After the memorial service, his father was not spoken of again. Then, when he was a father, one of his daughters had an eating disorder. In his despair and his pain he decided to seek help in attending an Alanon meeting. It was through that group that he became familiar with the slogan "let go and let God." He explains it as meaning to "let go of the dark, which you wrap yourself in like a straitjacket, and let in the light. Stop trying to protect, to rescue, to judge, to manage the lives around you— your children's lives, the lives of your husband, your wife, your friends—because that is just what you are powerless to do. Remember that the lives of other people are not your business. They are their business. They are God's business because they all have God whether they use the word God or not. Even your own life is not your business. It also is God's business. Leave it to God." "Let go and let God," was for Peggy a term that con- tributed to coming to know herself and to ultimately trust in a Higher Power for her own sense of fulfillment and for the well- being of her daughters. In attending AA meetings, Peggy began to speak her truth, to tell her secrets, to come to a point of accepting who she was, including the pain of her childhood, the anguish of being an alcoholic, and the freedom in knowing who she was.

In her second interview, Peggy was very weak and only able to speak in a very soft voice. Two of her three daughters were present. When asked about the spiritual dimension she said, "My experience of the spiritual is different every day. My sense of the spiritual increases from day to day, it's dynamic, it's changing. I think it's stronger today than it was when we spoke two weeks ago."

Through the course of her later years, Peggy came to accept who she was. She also grew to appreciate that her Higher Power accepted her unconditionally. This provided great solace for her. Is that an integrated process? Is it only in accepting ourselves fully that we are able to give that attribute to the Higher Power as well? For some people, living with a terminal illness means they pay attention to an inner voice, a voice that guides them to acknowledge the stranger within, the person they might have ignored prior to learning about their illness. It changes their psychological, and for some, their spiritual consciousness.

It seems that knowing one has a terminal illness affects one's consciousness; it's a process of transition from an outward journey to an inward journey. Knowing one has a terminal illness beckons one to move from the unconsciousness of the familiar to a new consciousness required to exist in the unfamiliar, from the superficiality of routine to a deeper attention of the soul.

Brent's Story

As you recall, Brent was a man in his thirties who had several hospital admissions through the course of his illness. During one of those admissions he had a near-death experience that had a profound effect on him. Until that point in time, Brent was living with a stranger. That stranger was himself. The near-death experience altered his sense of the spiritual and ultimately altered his sense of himself: "I'm much more spiritual now than I ever was before because I do believe that I saw and did things that only someone who comes within a fraction of a second of remaining on the other side could do . . . I remember being very content there and very happy, even though I was very, very sick." In that context, Brent began to suspend judgment, to listen to his inner voice, a voice that seemed to have been mute for decades. In paying attention to the voice he became a stranger to those around him, and less of a stranger to himself.

For Brent, forgiving himself and others was identified as a key element of spirituality, as was addressing the issue of God.

> Everything you've ever done in your life. Forgiveness, regret, forgiving those that you think have done something to you and forgiving yourself for things you think you've done. Dealing with spirituality, dealing with God for the first time in my life, I decided that I had to either believe in God or I didn't. I prayed.

In *The Tibetan Book of Living and Dying*, Sogyal Rinpoche states that "Not everyone believes in a formal religion, but nearly everyone believes in forgiveness. Forgiveness exists in the nature of God; it is already there. God has already forgiven you, for God is forgiveness itself. But can you forgive yourself? That's the real question . . . All religions stress the power of forgiveness, and this power is never more necessary, nor more deeply felt, than when someone is dying. Through forgiving and being forgiven, we purify ourselves of the darkness of what we have done, and prepare ourselves most completely for the journey through death." (p. 213)

Spirituality for Brent meant accepting others for who they are in a nonjudgmental way.

. . . no one ever said to me "you need to ask for forgive-ness for your sins." There was no judgment about lifestyle, there was nothing like that.

I believe in a Higher Power now like I've never believed before . . . I believe in God now. Not that I did-n't believe in Him before but I believe that there is so much more out there than I'd ever thought. By praying and asking for forgiveness and giving forgiveness I made a deal. I would never take my own life now. I know it's a gift. I'll never be the same. I mean, no matter how bad my life may seem, I can always find something that makes me feel fortunate and I don't know if that's spiri-tuality. I just have this belief that things are as they are meant to be. They will work out. There's no religion in particular but when you pray and your prayer is answered, you have got to believe that something, some-how happened here.

Brent confirmed that for him spirituality pertained to a Higher Power, a belief in God, in requesting and granting forgiveness, and in prayer. In his experience, it was not associated with a particular religion. He also felt that it provided a connection to those who had died before him.

In his sense of the spiritual, he realized that life is worth living and fun, that death is not an awful thing, and that he had a sense of a spirit being with him, meaning he felt he was never alone.

I felt that somehow I'd been given a gift . . . maybe I was just learning that life was worth living and was fun. Even on oxygen and unable to walk, it was better than death, but that death was not a bad thing either. That's the other thing that I found out, that death was not such an awful thing . . . I'm never alone any more.

The experience of the spiritual included strength, love, acceptance and presence.

My Maker . . . was powerful, it was strong and it was full of love and it loved me unconditionally. In spite of being a homosexual and having HIV and not having fulfilled "a life of Christian duty," it loved me unconditionally and that all I had to do was ask, "Please help me," and it did.

In that context, he, too, found a source of strength and a freedom from the fear of death.

I mean of all these things, where do I have the strength to go on? I believe that comes from within, from knowing now that I'm not alone, that there is, there is Someone there and whether we call Him Allah, Buddha, Jesus, whatever you want to call Him, there is Someone there and I think that I would not have ever known that . . . I'm no longer afraid of dying.

Acknowledging a Higher Power required courage on Brent's part in that it resulted in his being ostracized by his peers.

. . . I tell you, admitting to someone that you believe in a Higher Power in a gay community is not easy, 'cause right away they think you're, you're strange. They don't want to have anything to do with you.

In the context of the unconditional love experienced from the Higher Power, Brent was able to learn to love himself unconditionally. Like Peggy, he also gave up control to the Higher Power and in so doing, recognized that healing of the soul precedes healing of the body. For him, healing of the soul included healing wounds of childhood and adulthood, and ridding himself of self-hatred. The Higher Power was seen as the source of self-love.

> You can give up or you can put your faith into someone, into someone or something to help you along and that's what I did. I sort of let God take control. Along with the Higher Power loving you unconditionally, you have to love yourself unconditionally, meaning warts and all. No one's perfect. There's no reason in the world why I'm no more deserving than anyone else—to be treated well, to succeed and to get healthier. We're all deserving of love and we're all deserving to heal, but you know, healing is something that has to happen in the soul first, I think, and then the body heals. It's funny how you have to heal all those old wounds as a child and as a young adult, and in my case having been a gay man, and a gay young man and a gay prepubescent boy, you grow up with all this self-hate. Once you accept all of that is just bull, you learn to love yourself as an individual. Then you can start to heal. I don't think you can heal until those issues happen and once you love yourself for who you are.

For Brent, acknowledging the spiritual had to do with his personal history, his fears and his self-loathing—his sense that

although he was seen as a mistake of nature by others, that that
was not the case.

> . . . end-of-life issues, especially for gay men, that's what
> I'm speaking of, has to do with God. They're afraid of
> hell, they're afraid of the brimstone and of all of the pun-
> ishment for being bad, so their fear of death is terrifying.
> It's like it's not going to be good, it's going to be awful,
> this is a punishment, that I'm paying for my sins, I'm pay-
> ing for what I've been, what I am. You could help them
> by explaining that we're all equal, we're all loved, we're
> all okay. Help them walk through that understanding
> because there's often confusion. I like the idea of saying
> we're created in His image. Therefore if we're in His
> image, we're okay. If we weren't we wouldn't be here,
> pure and simple . . . they should be accepted and loved
> for what they are.

For Brent, the experience of dying was the ultimate "wake up"
call, spiritually and psychologically. Through physical unconsciousness, he awoke to a greater psychological consciousness
and spiritual awareness.

> It wasn't just wake up so you can speak to people but it
> was like wake up; this is your life now . . . It was like
> being reborn. It was truly being given an opportunity to
> understand that we all control our destiny to some
> point by the way we behave in our present life. A lot of
> people go through life pretending they're something
> they're not.

In truly knowing one's self and in believing in a Higher Power, one finds resolution, completeness, wholeness and integrity.

> . . . like all of a sudden all the pieces fit. People all go around searching for what'll make them happy, drugs, cars, sex, whatever it is . . . But once you find and put the pieces of this puzzle together, you no longer need these outside things to make you feel complete. You feel much better about being alive than ever before . . . understand that the wholeness that a person achieves when they start to believe in, in a Higher Power, makes them a better person.

Peggy and Brent were able to take the fragments of their past and hold them in the present. They took the good, the bad and the ugly of their lives and worked to integrate those truths into understanding who they had become. As they integrated their fragments into a new wholeness, they experienced a sense of healing. For Peggy and Brent, authenticity prevailed. Authenticity brought them a deep sense of connection to their inner spirits, to the spirits of people who were important to them, and to the Greater Spirit of the Universe. They were not cured of the disease process going on within them, and yet they felt healed. They moved from despair toward integrity, from psychological unconsciousness to wisdom, from fear to compassion.

How do I change my consciousness, my awareness, my attention? In silence, with questions, listening. Some other ways it happens are in discussions of meaningful topics, in group work, in journal-writing, in therapy, and in contemplative practices. People can reflect on themes such as the ones listed below and on the following pages. These are not questions that will provoke easy or straightforward answers, but space is provided here in case jotting down your thoughts as they occur to you helps you focus on this process.

• Who am I?

• Why are we here?

• Is there life after death? If so, what is it like?

- What does reincarnation mean to me?

- What is our/my purpose in life? What is the meaning of life?

- What makes my heart sing?

- What is my sorrow, my grief, my pain?

- Is the religious/spiritual tradition I grew up in the same as what I now practice? If so, why is it important to me? If not, what did I gain from it (if anything) and why is it not important to me?

- What does death mean to me? What has the experience of dying and death been in my life?

- What does life mean to me?

- Do I know love?

- What do time and space mean to me?

....
....
....
....
....

- Is God, Goddess, Buddha, Shiva, Brahman, Vishnu, the Hidden Essence, a Higher Power important to me?

....
....
....
....
....
....
....

- If I knew I had hours, days, weeks, months or years of life remaining, how would I spend my time? Who would I spend my time with?

....
....
....
....
....
....
....
....

As stated at the beginning of this chapter, a spiritual journey calls one's whole being into question.

Be still
Suspend judgment
Listen
Be silent
Pay attention
Be awake
Know yourself

Meditation/Contemplative Practice

There are many forms of meditation. I suggest that you learn more about them. Many communities offer courses on the various forms of meditation. Some resources you might consider are:

Goldstein, Joseph and Kornfield, Jack (1987) *Seeking the Heart of Wisdom*, Boston: Shambhala Publications, Inc.

Keating, Thomas (1992) *Open Mind, Open Heart, The Contemplative Dimension of the Gospel*, New York: The Continuum Publishing Company.

Rinpoche, Sogyal (1992) *The Tibetan Book of Living and Dying*, New York: HarperCollins. (See chapter 5: Bringing the Mind Home (pp. 56–81)).

Schachter-Shalomi, Zalman and Miller, Ronald S. (1995) *From Ageing to Sage-ing, A Profound Vision of Growing Older*, New York: Warner Books, pp. 124–134.

References

Bradshaw, John. *Healing the Shame That Binds You.* Deerfield Beach: Health Communications, 1988.

Birren, James E., and Donna E. Deutchman. *Guiding Autobiography Groups for Older Adults: Exploring the Fabric of Life.* Baltimore: Johns Hopkins University Press, 1991.

Bowlby, John. *A Secure Base: Parent-Child Attachment and Healthy Human Development.* New York: Basic Books, 1988.

Buechner, Frederick. *Telling Secrets: A Memoir.* New York: HarperCollins, 1991.

Diggory, J. and D. Rotheman "Values Destroyed by Death." *Journal of Abnormal and Social Psychology* 63(1961): 205–210.

Erikson, Erik H. *Identity: A Life Cycle.* New York: W.W. Norton, 1980.

Herman, Judith. *Trauma and Recovery.* New York: Basic Books, 1992.

Hollis, James. *Creating a Life: Finding Your Individual Path.* Toronto: Inner City Books, 2000.

Hollis, James. *The Middle Passage: From Misery to Meaning in Midlife.* Toronto: Inner City Books, 1993.

Hollis, James. *Swamplands of the Soul: New Life in Dismal Places.* Toronto: Inner City Books, 1996.

Hollis, James. *Tracking the Gods: The Place of Myth in Modern Life.* Toronto: Inner City Books, 1995.

Jonsen, Albert, Mark Siegler and William J. Winslade. *Clinical Ethics, 3rd ed.* New York: McGraw-Hill, 1992.

Kenyon, Gary M., and William L. Randall. *Restorying Our Lives: Personal Growth Through Autobiographical Reflection.* New York: Praeger, 1997.

Kornfield, Jack. *A Path with Heart: A Guide Through the Perils and Promises of Spiritual Life.* New York: Bantam Books, 1993.

Kuhl, David. *What Dying People Want: Practical Wisdom for the End of Life*. Toronto: Doubleday Canada, 2002.

Kuhl, David and Patricia Wilensky, "Decision-Making at the End of Life: A Model Using an Ethical Grid and Principles of Group Process." *Journal of Palliative Medicine* 2, No. 1 (1999): 75–86.

Maslow, Abraham H. *Motivation and Personality, 2ⁿᵈ ed*. New York: Harper & Row Publishers, 1970.

Meninger, William A. *The Process of Forgiveness*. New York: Continuum, 1999.

Miller, Alice. *The Drama of a Gifted Child: The Search for the True Self*, revised ed. New York: BasicBooks, 1994.

Montagu, Ashley. *Touching: The Human Significance of the Skin, 3ʳᵈ ed*. New York: Harper & Row. 1986.

Moyers, Bill *Healing and the Mind*. New York: Doubleday, 1993.

Rinpoche, Sogyal. *The Tibetan Book of Living and Dying*. New York: HarperCollins, 1992.

Satir, Virginia, John Banmen, Jane Gerber, and Maria Gomori. *The Satir Model: Family Therapy and Beyond*. Palo Alta, California: Science and Behaviour Books, 1991.

Schachter-Shalomi, Zalman, and Miller, Ronald S. *From Age-ing to Sage-ing: A Profound Vision of Growing Older*. New York: Warner Books, 1995.

Spiegel, David, J.R. Bloom, and Irving Yalom. "Group Support for Patients with Metastatic Cancer." *Archives of General Psychiatry* 38 (May 1981): 527–533.

Thomas, Lewis. *The Youngest Science: Notes of a Medicine-Watcher*. New York: Bantam Books, 1983.

Toman, Walter. *Family Constellation: Its Effects on Personality and Social Behavior*. New York: Springer Publishing Company, 1976.

Wallen, J. "The Interpersonal Gap." *Interpersonal Communication Leaders Manual*, Charles Jung, Rosalie Howard, Ruth Emory and René Pino. Oregon: Northwest Regional Educational Laboratory, 1972.

Wilber, Ken. *Eye to Eye: The Quest for the New Paradigm*. New York: Anchor Books, 1983.

Yalom, Irvin D. *The Yalom Reader: Selections from the Work of a Master Therapist and Storyteller*. New York: Basic Books, 1998.

Resources

National Organizations

Canadian Caregiver Coalition
110 Argyle Avenue
Ottawa, ON K2P 1B3
Tel: 613–233–5694, ex. 2230
Toll free: 888–866–2273
Fax: 613–230–4376
Web: www.ccc-ccan.ca

Canadian Cancer Society
10 Alcorn Avenue, Suite 200
Toronto, ON M4V 3B1
Tel: 416–961–7223
Fax: 416–961–4189
Web: www.cancer.ca

Canadian Hospice Palliative Care Association
Annex B, Saint-Vincent Hospital
60 Cambridge Street North
Ottawa, ON K1R 7A5
Tel: 613–241–3663
Toll free: 1–800–668–2785
Fax: 613–241–3986
Web: www.chpca.net

Canadian Virtual Hospice
Web: www.virtualhospice.ca/
public/splash.asp

Caregiver Network Inc.
2 Oaklawn Gardens, Unit C
Toronto, ON M4V 2C6
Tel: 416–323–1090
Fax: 416–323–9422
Web: www.caregiver.on.ca

CATIE (Canadian AIDS Treatment Information Exchange)
555 Richmond Street W, Suite 505,
Box 1104
Toronto, ON M5V 3B1
Tel: 416–203–7122
Toll free: 1–800–263–1638
Fax: 416–203–8284
Web: www.catie.ca

Circle of Care
530 Wilson Avenue, 4th Floor
Toronto, ON M3H 1T6
Web: www.circleofcare.com/
home.html

Grief, Loss and Recovery
PO Box 581277
Minneapolis, MN 55458–1277
Toll free: 1–800–211–1202,
ext. 14436
Web: www.grieflossrecovery.com

Health Canada
Address Locator 0900C2
Ottawa, ON K1A 0K9

Web: www.hc-sc.gc.ca/index_e.html
Legacy Creations
Box 216
Sutton West, ON L0E 1R0
Web: www.emotionallegacy.com

MISS Foundation
P.O. Box 5333
Peoria, AZ 85385
Tel: 623–979–1000
Fax: 623–979–1001
Web: www.misschildren.org

Provincial Organizations

ALBERTA

Alberta Hospice Palliative Care Association
c/o Pilgrims Hospice Society, 9808
148 Street
Edmonton, AB T5N 3E8
Tel: 780–454–4848
Email: pcareab@telus.net

Calgary

Carewest Administrative Centre
1070 McDougall Road N.E.
Calgary, AB T2E 7Z2
Tel: 403–267–2900
Fax: 403–267–2968
Web: http://www.carewest.org/

Hospice Calgary
833–4 Avenue S.W., Suite 900
Calgary, AB T2P 3T5
Tel: 403–263–4525
Fax: 403–263–4524
Web: http://www.hospicecalgary.com

Edmonton

Capital Health Regional Palliative Care Program
Grey Nuns Community Hospital
5111, 1100 Youville Drive West
Edmonton, AB T6L 5X8
Tel: 780–450–7934
Fax: 780–450–7640
Web: www.palliative.org

Pilgrims Hospice Society
9808 148 Street
Edmonton, AB T5N 3E8
Tel: 780–413–9801
Fax: 780–413–9748
Email: hospice@telusplanet.net

Red Deer

David Thompson Health Region
2845 Bremner Avenue
Red Deer, AB T4R 1S2
Tel: 403–341–2411
Fax: 403–341–2196
Email: rkoshy@dthr.ab.ca

Red Deer Hospice Society
99 Arnot Avenue
Red Deer, AB T4R 3S6
Tel: 403–309–4344
Web: www.reddeerhospice.com

BRITISH COLUMBIA

BC Palliative Care Association
Room 502, Comox Building, 1081
Burrard Street
Vancouver, BC V6Z 1Y6
Tel: 604–806–8821
Toll free: 877–422–4722
Fax: 604–806–8822
Web: http://www.hospicebc.org/

Palliative Resource Centre of
British Columbia
Web: www.prbc.ca

Burnaby

TCM Telecare
250–4170 Still Creek Drive
Burnaby, BC V5C 6C6
Tel: 604–215–5106
Fax: 604–215–5105
Email: dmaccormack@telecare.ca

Surrey

Surrey Hospice Society
13857 - 68th Avenue
Surrey, BC V3W 2G9
Tel: 604–543–7006
Fax: 604–543–7008
Web: www.surreyhospice.com

Vancouver

Caregiver Support Program
3425 Crowley Drive
Vancouver, BC V5R 6G3
Tel: 604–877–4699
Fax: 604–872–2368
Email: kristen.farquharson@vch.ca

Peace of Mind Palliative Care
West 44th Avenue
Vancouver, BC V6M 2G2
Tel: 604–808–2475
Email: nicole@palliativecarebc.com

Victoria

Victoria Hospice Society
1952 Bay Street
Victoria, BC V8R 1J8
Tel: 250–370–8715
Fax: 250–370–8625
Web: http://www.victoriahospice.org/

MANITOBA

Hospice & Palliative Care
Manitoba
2109 Portage Avenue
Winnipeg, MB R3J 0L3
Tel: 204–889–8525
Toll free: 800–539–0295 (MB use
only)
Fax: 204–888–8874
Email: info@manitobahospice.mb.ca

Brandon

Brandon Regional Health Authority
Palliative Care Service
B-150 7th Street
Brandon, MB R7A 7M2
Tel: 204–571–8429
Fax: 204–726–5720
Email: brandonpalliative@yahoo.ca

W.A.T.C.H. WESTMAN
HOSPICE
Unit M, 435 Rosser Avenue
Brandon, MB R7A 6S2
Tel: 204–727–1745
Fax: 204–728–7835
Email: watch@mb.sympatico.ca

Winnipeg

Canadian Virtual Hospice
Rm PE450 - One Morley Avenue
Winnipeg, MB R3L 2P4
Tel: 204–475–1494
Toll free: 866–288–4803
Fax: 204–475–1497
Web: www.virtualhospice.ca

Winnipeg Regional Health
Authority Palliative Care
Sub-Program
A8024–409 Tache Avenue
Winnipeg, MB R2H 2A6

Tel: 204–237–2400
Fax: 204–237–9162
Web: www.palliative.info

NEW BRUNSWICK

New Brunswick Hospice Palliative Care Association
c/o 280 Connaught Street,
Apartment 24
Fredericton, NB E3B 2B4
Tel: 506–452–9310
Email: psomerville@nb.aibn.com

Fredericton

Dr. Everett Chalmers Hospital Palliative Care Unit
DECH, 700 Priestman Street, P.O. Box 9000
Fredericton, NB E3B 5N5
Tel: 506–452–5364
Email: sydgrant@nb.sympatico.ca

Moncton

South-East Regional Health Authority
135 MacBeath Avenue
Moncton, NB E1C 6Z8
Tel: 506–867–6500
Fax: 506–867–6509
Email: pamcquin@serha.ca

Saint John

Hospice Palliative Care Centre
3B North, Saint John Regional Hospital, 400 University Avenue
Saint John, NB E2L 4L2
Tel: 1–866–666–7423
Fax: 506–632–5593
Web: www.hospicesj.com

Palliative Care Unit, Saint John Regional Hospital
3B North, Saint John Regional Hospital, P.O. Box 2100
Saint John, NB E2L 4L2
Tel: 506–648–6155
Fax: 506–648–7086
Email: maxde@reg2.health.nb.ca

NEWFOUNDLAND

Newfoundland & Labrador Palliative Care Association
100 Forrest Road
St. John's, NF A1A 1E5
Tel: 709–777–8638
Fax: 709–777–8635
Web: www.nlpca.info

Corner Brook

WHCC Palliative Care Service (Western Newfoundland)
1 Brookfield Avenue
Corner Brook, NF A2H 6J7
Tel: 709–637–5000
Email: palliativecare@healthwest.nf.ca

St. John's

Palliative Care Health Care Corporation of St. John's
100 Forrest Road
St. John's, NF A1A 1E5
Tel: 709–777–8611
Fax: 709–777–8635
Email: LaurieAnne.OBrien@hccsj.nf.ca

VON St. John's Branch
39 Campbell Avenue
St. John's, NF A1E 2Z3
Tel: 709–726–8597
Fax: 709–726–4228
Email: von@nf.aibn.com

NOVA SCOTIA

**Nova Scotia Hospice Palliative
Care Association**
c/o Colchester Regional Hospital
Truro, NS B2H 5A1
Tel: 902–893–7171
Fax: 902–893–7172
Web: http://www.nshpca.ca

Halifax

**Capital District Integrated
Palliative Care Program**
1278 Tower Road, 7A Centennial
Building, Room 054, Victoria
Halifax, NS B3H 2Y9
Tel: 902–473–7776
Fax: 902–473–3103
Email: pauline.fowlie@cdha.
nshealth.ca

Hospice Society of Greater Halifax
P.O. Box 33076
Halifax, NS B3L 4T6
Tel: 902–446–0929
Web: www.hospicehalifax.com

New Glasgow

Aberdeen Palliative Care Society
835 East River Road
New Glasgow, NS B2H 3S6
Tel: 902–752–7600 Ext. 4190
Fax: 702–755–2356
Email: p.hermillon@ns.sympatico.ca

**Pictou Country District
Health Authority**
835 East River Road
New Glasgow, NS B2H 3S6
Tel: 902–752–7600 Ext. 4190
Fax: 902–755–2356
Email:
dmacdonald@pcdha.ns.health.ca

NORTHWEST TERRITORIES

Hay River

**Hay River Community Health
Board**
3 Gaetz Drive
Hay River, NT X0E 0R8
Tel: 867–874–7201
Fax: 867–874–7211
Email: laurette_hamilton@gov.nt.ca

NUNAVUT

Coral Harbour

**Nunavut Home & Community
Care**
Box 194
Coral Harbour, NU X0C 0C0
Tel: 867–925–9916
Fax: 867–925–8380
Email: bnielsen@gov.nu.ca

ONTARIO

Hospice Association of Ontario
Suite 201, 27 Carlton Street
Toronto, ON M5B 1L2
Tel: 416–304–1477
Toll free: 800–349–3111
Fax: 416–304–1479
Web: www.hospice.on.ca

Ontario Palliative Care Association
194 Eagle Street
Newmarket, ON L3Y 1J6
Tel: 905–954–0938
Toll free: 888–379–6666
Fax: 905–954–0939
Email: opca@neptune.on.ca

Hamilton

Dr. Bob Kemp Hospice
1 Wardrope Avenue
Hamilton, ON L8G 1R9
Tel: 905–664–4652
Toll free: 800–449–3440
Fax: 905–664–9834
Web: www.kemphospice.org

Hamilton Hospice Palliative
Care Network
310 Limeridge Road West
Hamilton, ON L9C 2V2
Tel: 905–526–3612
Fax: 905–574–6154
Email: janet.jones@hamilton.
ccac-ont.ca

Mississauga

Hospice of Peel
855 Matheson Blvd.
Mississauga, ON L6W 4L6
Tel: 905–712–8119
Fax: 905–712–4029
Web: www.hospiceofpeel.com
VON Peel Branch
6745 Century Avenue Suite 5
Mississauga, ON L5N 7K2
Tel: 905–821–3242
Fax: 905–821–7100
Email: burtons@von.ca

Ottawa

The Hospice at May Court
114 Cameron Avenue
Ottawa, ON K1S 0X1
Tel: 613–260–2906
Web: www.hospicemaycourt.com

Lamplight Palliative Care
14 Castleton Street
Ottawa, ON K2G 5M7
Tel: 613–298–9446
Web: lamplightpalliativecare.ca

ParaMed Home Health Care
295 Wolfe Street
Ottawa, ON N6B 2C4
Tel: 519–433–2222
Fax: 519–433–5588
Web: www.extendicare.com

Toronto

Bayview Community Hospice
210–40 Wynford Drive
Toronto, ON M3C 1J5
Tel: 416–385–8885
Fax: 416–385–8887
Web: www.bayviewhospice.org

Calea Palliative Care
2785 Skymark Unit 2
Toronto, ON L4W 4Y3
Tel: 416–238–1903
Fax: 905–238–4898
Email: palliativecare@calea.ca

The Dorothy Ley Hospice
3 - 170 Sherway Drive
Toronto, ON M9C 1A6
Tel: 416–626–0116
Fax: 416–626–7285
Web: www.dlhospice.org

Hospice Palliative Care Network Project
700 University Avenue, 3rd Floor,
Suite 3000
Toronto, ON M5G 1Z5
Tel: 416–586–4800 Ext. 7884
Fax: 416–586–4804
Web: www.tlcpc.org

Trinity Home Hospice
Suite 1102 - 25 King Street West
Toronto, ON M5L 1G3
Tel: 416–364–1666
Fax: 416–364–2231
Web: www.thh.on.ca

VHA Home HealthCare
170 Merton Street
Toronto, ON M4L 1N3
Tel: 416–489–2500
Toll free: 1–888–314–6622
Fax: 416–489–7533
Web: www.vha.on.ca

PRINCE EDWARD ISLAND

Hospice Palliative Care Association of Prince Edward Island
5 Brighton Road
Charlottetown, PE C1A 8T6
Tel: 902–368–4498
Fax: 902–368–4095
Web: www.hospicepei.ca

Charlottetown

Queens County
Queen Elizabeth Hospital
Charlottetown, PE C1A 8T5
Tel: 902–894–2148
Web: www.hospicepei.ca

Summerside

East Prince Health Palliative Care Program
310 Brophy Avenue
Summerside, PE C1N 5N4
Tel: 902–432–2709
Fax: 902–888–8349
Email: carowswell@ihis.org

QUEBEC

Réseau de soins palliatifs du Québec
500, rue Sherbrooke Ouest, bureau 900
Montreal, QC H3A 3C6
Tel: 514–282–3808
Fax: 514–844–7556
Web: www.reseaupalliatif.org

Montreal

Sir Mortimer B. Davis Jewish General Hospital
3755 Chemin de la cote Ste-Cathe
Montreal, QC H3T 1E2
Tel: 514–340–8222
Email: blapoint@onc.jgh.mcgill.ca

Equinoxe LifeCare Solutions
4823 Sherbrooke Street West
Montreal, QC H3Z 1G7
Tel: 514–935–2600
Toll free: 877–935–2600
Fax: 514–935–0230
Web: www.equinoxe.ca

Quebec City

CHUQ
11, côte du Palais
Québec, QC G1R 2J6
Tel: 418–525–4444
Fax: 418–691–5792
Email: Louis.Roy@chuq.qc.ca

Saguenay

Programme de soins palliatifs CSSSC
305 St-Vallier
Saguenay (arr. Chicoutimi), QC
G7H 5H6
Tel: 418–541–1000 Ext. 2927
Email: johanne.theriault@ssss.
gouv.qc.ca

SASKATCHEWAN

Saskatchewan Hospice Palliative Care Association
Box 37053
Regina, SK S4S 7K3
Tel: 306–585–2871
Fax: 306–790–8634
Web: www.saskpalliativecare.com

Prince Albert

Home Care (Prince Albert, SK)
196 9th Street East
Prince Albert, SK S6V 0X5
Tel: 306–922–2969
Fax: 306–763–4472
Email: psayer@paphr.sk.ca

PAPHR
1200 24th Street West
Prince Albert, SK S6V 5T4
Tel: 306–765–6000 Ext. 6255
Toll free: 306–765–6000 Ext. 6235
Fax: 306–765–6000 Ext. 6237
Web: www.paphr.sk.ca

Regina

Regina Health District Palliative Care Services
4F - 4101 Dewdney Avenue
Regina, SK S4T 1A5

Tel: 306–766–2665
Fax: 306–766–2588
Email: vclark@reginahealth.sk.ca

Regina Palliative Care Inc.
4F - 4101 Dewdney Avenue
Regina, SK S4T 1A5
Tel: 306–766–2300
Fax: 306–766–2588
Email: mlynch@reginahealth.sk.ca

Saskatoon

Saskatoon Palliative Care Services
1702 - 20th Street West
Saskatoon, SK S7M 0Z9
Tel: 306–655–5868
Fax: 306–655–5918
Web: www.sdh.sk.ca/palliative

YUKON

Whitehorse

Hospice Yukon
409 Jarvis
Whitehorse, YT Y1A 2H4
Tel: 867–667–7429
Fax: 867–633–4683
Email:
hospiceadmin@whtvcable.com

Yukon Home Care Program
3168–3rd Avenue
Whitehorse, YT Y1A 1G3
Tel: 867–667–5774
Fax: 867–393–6328
Email: gail.chester@gov.yk.ca

Acknowledgments

I begin by thanking the people who participated in the study on which this book is based. I dedicate this work to them. I thank them for their time, their stories, and their insights, which helped me to deepen my understanding of what it means to face death and embrace life.

I am grateful for the support I received through St. Paul's Hospital, Providence Health Care and the Department of Family Practice, Faculty of Medicine, University of British Columbia. In that regard, I especially thank Dr. Akber Mithani, Vice President, Medicine at Providence Health Care and Dr. Robert Woollard, Head, Department of Family Practice, University of British Columbia for their ongoing support of my work.

I thank my colleagues Linda Bullock and Linda MacNutt for their collaborative spirit, supportive attitudes and challenging of ideas on a daily basis. I thank Dr. Hilary Pearson for her ideas in developing and strengthening the concepts and applications in the book. Thanks to Dr.

Douglas Cave for many discussions about this work and for the opportunity to integrate some of the exercises into his classes at UBC.

I thank Denise Bukowski, my literary agent, for believing in this work and my first book, and her assistant Jackie Joiner for working with me to produce a companion book that would be of practical application to assist the reader in understanding what dying people want. I also thank Amy Black, my editor at Doubleday Canada, for her incredible patience, kindness, encouragement and perseverance in seeing this project to its conclusion.

Thanks to David Williams for the time he spent in reading and correcting the document. Thanks also to Dr. Marv Westwood for being a great teacher and friend. Thanks to Dianne Westwood for shared insights over the years and for assistance in details pertaining to the finishing touches of the manuscript. I thank my brother, Robert, for believing in me. I thank my young friends (Sean, Mikey, Shannon, Megan, Lexi, Maddi, and Taya) who, during this past summer, kept humour in my life at the cottage when efforts to complete the manuscript eroded my ability to laugh at times. To that list of friends I add Jennifer and Sarah who have the wonderful ability to keep a song in their hearts year round and who have taught me a great deal about embracing life.

I thank Jean, who embraces life with me, for her tireless 'editing' of ideas, words and concepts that comprised this work. And more importantly, I thank her for all the counsel (an endless conversation that seems all too short), the listening and the love she has given me through the past decades of our shared lives.